D1566564

Love Poems by Pedro Salinas

[signature: Pedro Salinas]

LOVE POEMS BY
PEDRO SALINAS
. . . .

My		Letter
Voice	*&*	Poems
Because		to
of You		Katherine

. . . .

Translated with an Introduction by
WILLIS BARNSTONE

with a Foreword by JORGE GUILLÉN

and an Afterword by ENRIC BOU

The University of Chicago Press
CHICAGO AND LONDON

Born in Madrid in 1891 and a leading figure in Spain's literary scene, PEDRO SALINAS was a literature professor, poet, short story writer, novelist, dramatist, essayist, and literary critic who taught at the University of Seville, the Sorbonne, Cambridge, and elsewhere in Europe, and spent much of his life in the United States, at Middlebury College, Wellesley College, and Johns Hopkins University, among other institutions. He is the author of nine books of poems, six of which appeared in English translation, three during his lifetime. He died in Boston in 1951.

Widely recognized as a leading American translator, poet, and biblical scholar, WILLIS BARNSTONE is currently Distinguished Professor Emeritus of Comparative Literature and Spanish at Indiana University. Among his many publications are *The Poetics of Translation: History, Theory, Practice* (1993), *Life Watch: Poems* (2003), *The Gnostic Bible* (2003), *The Gnostic Bible: Gnostic Texts of Mystical Wisdom from the Ancient and Medieval Worlds* (2006), and *The Restored New Testament: A New Translation with Commentary, Including the Gnostic Gospels Thomas, Mary, and Judas* (2009).

ENRIC BOU is professor and chair of Hispanic studies at Brown University. Among his many publications are two editions of the letters of Pedro Salinas, an edition of the letters of Katherine Whitmore, and, most recently, *Daliccionario: Objetos, mitos y simbolos de Salvador Dalí* (2004) and Pedro Salinas's *Obras Completas* (2007).

The University of Chicago Press, Chicago 60637
The University of Chicago Press, Ltd., London
© 2010 by The University of Chicago
All rights reserved. Published 2010
Printed in the United States of America

Spanish poems copyright © The Estate of Pedro Salinas.
All rights reserved.

19 18 17 16 15 14 13 12 11 10   1 2 3 4 5

ISBN-13: 978-0-226-73426-2 (cloth)
ISBN-10: 0-226-73426-9 (cloth)

The University of Chicago Press gratefully acknowledges the generous support of the Program for Cultural Cooperation between Spain's Ministry of Culture and United States universities toward the publication of this book.

Illustrations on pages ii and iii: Pedro Salinas (ca. 1920s) and Salinas's autograph (n.d.). Courtesy the Heirs of Pedro Salinas.

Library of Congress Cataloging-in-Publication Data

Salinas, Pedro, 1892–1951.
[Poems. English. Selections. 2010]
Love poems by Pedro Salinas : my voice because of you, and letter poems to Katherine / Pedro Salinas ; translated with an introduction by Willis Barnstone ; with a foreword by Jorge Guillén and an afterword by Enric Bou.
p. cm.
Parallel text in English and Spanish; "Letter poems to Katherine" in English.
Includes bibliographical references and index.
ISBN-13: 978-0-226-73426-2 (cloth : alk. paper)
ISBN-10: 0-226-73426-9 (cloth : alk. paper)
I. Guillén, Jorge, 1893–1984. II. Barnstone, Willis, 1927– III. Bou, Enric. IV. Title.
PQ6635.A32A2 2010b
861'.62—dc22

2009026128

♾ The paper used in this publication meets the minimum requirements of the American National Standard for Information Sciences—Permanence of Paper for Printed Library Materials, ANSI Z39.48-1992.

CONTENTS

FOREWORD (1976)

· I ·

The work of Pedro Salinas reaches its summit in the theme of love. Has there been any love poetry written in the twentieth century more important than *My Voice Because of You*?

Lovers live alone, seeking and finding each other, happy and anguished, in their own insular spheres. It is always like that. Are there any lovers who are not, or do not wish to be, the sole inhabitants of an island closed off to the rest of the world? For they are the world. This is not poetry of extravagant love but of the most normal love in a completely normal story, and the story is confined to situations of fervid feeling that never slide into sentimentality. They unfold in an analytical description that is deeply thought and felt: thought, passion, tenderness, and sensuality fuse together perfectly in a poetry of intensely uniform words. The voice because of love is passionate as a result of anxious searching. Where does the constant hunger come from? There is no social conflict. At such times society does not exist. Is there an internal conflict? No. The lover begins from love—a love he had once—toward the *amada* (the woman loved), toward the best possible *amada*.

· II ·

I, you: that is all. Salinas completes, intensifies, elevates the situation without weakening its normality:

> It's that I want to take out
> of you the best you.

Jorge Guillén was professor at the Sorbonne, Paris, at the University of Oxford, and at Wellesley College. Recipient of the prestigious Miguel de Cervantes, prize, Gullén was one of the great symbolist poets of the twentieth century. His comments in this foreword, which has been reprinted from the State University of New York Press edition of 1976, refer only to Willis Barnstone's English translation of *La voz a ti debida*. At the time, Guillén was unaware of the letter poems to Katherine Whitmore. The 1976 English translations of *La voz* cited by Guillén have been updated to match the translations in the 2010 edition.

And so the woman—nameless now—becomes a you that implies some kind of mysterious Beyond. Then he discards the figure of a love who might become a deity, under whose power he might suffer. The *I* and *you* share the atmosphere of an Eros that is not a god but a newly created circumference of love. The "first trembling" is immediately confirmed. It is a Genesis with its primal freshness:

> What a sinless day!
> Foam, hour after hour,
> indefatigably

It is not a garden. It is a beach. And suddenly there is a felicitous liveliness:

> Yes, everything in excess:
> light, life, the sea!
> All plural, plural,
> lights, lives and seas.

The lovers give themselves

> blind—
> to a vast risky depth [that
> sings]:
> *This is still nothing.*
> *Look deeply in you. There's more.*

The heart hurls itself into this quest with pleasant and painful hunger, far from any simple cerebral entertainment. Of course these anxieties are both felt and thought. In lines already famous, he writes:

> To live I don't want
> islands, palaces, towers.
> What steeper joy
> than living in pronouns!

Pronouns, the skeletal grammatical word. The ingenious poet uses them with irony. Are the pronouns *I, you,* metaphysical entities? These monosyllabic condensations reveal the lovers' profound essence that will always exist. The lover says with the greatest simplicity:

I want you.

It is love that discloses—and creates—the two lovers. A new *I* wants to become a new *you*. *I, you*: the relationship of all lovers, which in this instance acquires extraordinary height and depth.

· III ·

> I want you pure, free,
> irreducible: you.

A chimera of Platonic perfection is not sought here. Rather, what is longed for is the most profound, secret *you* that love can reveal and exalt, as if that love were dreamt in the "pure, unmoving center in you." This moment of ecstatic calm implies a now unreal hyperbole of the quest that no single plenitude or intoxication can satisfy. It is the extreme Beyond of great demanding love. The lover is not wildly desirous because of the Idea of an inaccessible Laura. His anguished longing corresponds precisely to the reality enjoyed and suffered. It corresponds to plain realism. Will the restlessness ever end? We read: "I don't know where to find you," where to find the *you* that the lover pursues; and the speaker continues, with a simple hyperbole: "shouting or with only the wings of silence" as he pursues the other being who is sinking into herself:

> to ask you to love me
> is to ask it for you
> . . . .
> to go
> even beyond
> ultimate
> mines of your being,

the true, the truest ones. So there is a kind of gravitational pull toward the earth:

> . . . Look for weights,
> the deepest in you, so they can drag you down
> to the great center where I wait for you.
> Total love, wanting each other like masses.

Idealism? There is no conflict between passion and behavior. Rather, a vibrating tension: the aim of surpassing the physical zone in the physical zone itself. There is no idyll or drama here, but a quivering loving fullness: "the irreducible you, a naked certain Venus." Nothing is avoided.

> I don't want you to go,
> pain, last form
> of loving. . . .

The story already has a past:

> we have lived together
> in fragile delicate worlds.

Separation reduces the lovers to their own shadows. Remember the last extraordinary poem of *My Voice Because of You*:

> Do you hear how they beg for realities,
> those disheveled terrible beasts,
> they, the shadows that we both forge
> in this great bed of distances?

The question is energetically directed to the absent, remote woman (*amada*). In a poem of absence. A concrete demand for "realities" rises from the poem. All phantasmagoria is now excluded. And the end:

> . . . return again
> to a mortal and pink body
> where love invents its infinity.

"Corporality" is an abstract noun, yet not a dry concept, thanks to the rose color that evokes the image of a gloriously naked body lying down, "O, mortal" body with its melancholy perspective. The very serene and tender inclination to the concrete slips in where love invents its infinity. A Platonic Idea never hangs over the lovers like a Holy Ghost. Following his profane path a poet today cannot emulate Saint John of the Cross. The journey is taken, knowing that "Infinity" station is never reached. Love traces out the route, that's all: road, "method," no round trip—toward a horizontal nakedness, under a sky that contains all and has no end.

The poetry of Salinas perfectly embodies the sinuosity of his thought-feeling. The rational thread is never lost, and he finds the necessary means to make diction explicit. Images and explanations do not impede the course and, if needed, they produce their own explanations. In short, who but an obtuse critic could reduce to reason a whole poetic world? In this case we have the text of the first poet recreated by the second, Willis Barnstone, a poet extremely sensitive to ancient and modern poetry, the interpreter of The Song of Songs, Sappho, Saint John of the Cross, and other diverse figures, among whom the most recent are Antonio Machado and Mao Zedong, and who has the insight of a truly modern poet and critic.

Jorge Guillén (1893–1984)

ACKNOWLEDGMENTS (1976)

The poetry of Pedro Salinas lends itself to modern translation and more so than that of most of his contemporaries. Obviously this English version was done because of the value of the poem. But I should also acknowledge that I am repaying a debt to Pedro Salinas and his family, which back in 1947 opened the Spanish world to me. Professor Juan Marichal at Harvard, editor of the first *Poesías completas*, has always given much appreciated encouragement, and his wife, Solita, daughter of Pedro Salinas and editor of the 1971 text of *La voz*, has been extraordinarily helpful. She went over each poem of the first edition meticulously and saved the manuscript, not from unwarranted poetic freedoms but from many mistakes of interpretation of Pedro Salinas's subtly composed poems. Finally, Jorge Guillén, the great Spanish poet, has once again written about his friend Pedro Salinas, as he must know Salinas would be doing for him, were he alive today.* When I asked don Jorge for some introductory pages, his answer was true to his affirmative *Cántico*: "Si no tuviera ganas, lo haría" (If I did not feel like doing it, I would do it, and since I very much want to, you will have it in a month). My thanks to all.

Willis Barnstone

---

*See note in the foreword.

Pedro Salinas and friends (1933). *Front row, left to right*: Salinas, Ignacio Sánchez Mejías, and Jorge Guillén. *Back row, left to right*: Antonio Marichalar, José Bergamin, Corpus Barga, Vincente Aleixandre, Federico García Lorca, and Dámaso Alonso. Courtesy the Heirs of Pedro Salinas.

In 1898 Spain was ingloriously defeated in a war with the United States. The last illusion of empire vanished. But with this national disaster came an intellectual, artistic, and political awakening among novelists, poets, essayists, and philosophers known as the Generation of 1898, a movement that restored Spain to international prominence in the arts. About this Generation no one wrote more lucidly than Pedro Salinas in his volume *Literatura española siglo XX* (Spanish literature of the twentieth century). Salinas looked high and low. He spoke of the lowly but "patrician dignity" of the Castilian peasant, and he chronicled the work of the Generation's leaders: the grand poet Antonio Machado; the novelist Pío Baroja, whom Hemingway declared his master; the essayist Azorín, who gave the movement its name; and José Ortega y Gassett and Miguel de Unamuno, its philosophers and guides.

Pedro Salinas began to write and publish his own work two decades after the tumultuous Generation of '98. He was associated with a group of Spanish poets called the Generation of 1927, which included Rafael Alberti, Federico García Lorca, Jorge Guillén, Luis Cernuda, and Vicente Aleixandre. The youngest of the group, Miguel Hernández, the magnificent surreal and committed poet of light and darkness, was only thirty-one when he died of tuberculosis in 1942 in a Franco prison.[1] This grouping of friends was as brilliant as it was diverse and eclectic. In their totality they represented a renaissance of verse unseen since the golden age when Spain was the dominant power in Europe and the Americas. In that golden age (*siglo de oro*) of the sixteenth and seventeenth centuries, we have mysterious El Greco, master Diego Velazquez, giant Miguel de Cervantes, abundant Lope de Vega, and mystical Saint John of the Cross.

Like other vanguard movements in Europe, the Generation of '27 poets rejected immediate ancestors, except for Antonio Machado (1875–1939)

---

1. There is a strange, sad justice that today one of the important new universities in Spain is the Miguel Hernández University, with branches in four cities of the nation.

and Juan Ramón Jiménez (1981–58).[2] Machado was a model and friend of the younger emerging poets, as was Juan Ramón, whose late naked free verse and nimble music echoes in Salinas's minimalist poetry. The main focus of the Generation's gaze was on the European avant-garde, and especially French surrealism, which the young Vicente Aleixandre, García Lorca, and Pablo Neruda (for years in Madrid) got from France. Here was an unusual twist in world poetry where the disciples were to achieve greater mastery, fame, and influence than the formal inventors of the movement.[3]

The Generation poets also went centuries back to find models in their own literature. In doing so they made alliances not only with baroque Luis de Góngora (1561–1627), whose name favored their banner, but with the earliest anonymous Castilian ballads, and Galician and Andalusian folksong. Lorca was fascinated by gypsy and Arabic lyrics. In his last volume, which has an Arabic title (*Diván del Tamarit*) published in Sevilla in 1936 a few months after his execution, Lorca's poems followed the old Arabic forms of the *ghazal* and *qasida*. His fellow Andalusian, Manuel de Falla (1876–1946), a modern composer trained in Paris, chose to distill Andalusian folk music into his ballets and suites.

All these fresh raids on the past gave a universal freshness and modernity to this gathering of Spanish artists in the first half of the twentieth century. In music we have Manuel de Falla, Enrique Granados, Pablo Casals, Andrés Segovia. An array of amazing painters and filmmakers went to Paris: Joan Miro, Juan Gris, Salvador Dali, and Luis Buñuel. Their most important expatriate was the ultra Spaniard from Málaga and Barcelona, Pablo Picasso, who for nearly a century led movements of modern painting, sculpture, and ceramics as he handsomely exploited earlier periods from Egypt, black Africa, Greece, the far East, and wherever his renovating eye focused.[4]

2. When Jiménez was awarded the Nobel in literature in 1958, the Royal Swedish Academy made the unusual declaration that in honoring Juan Ramón Jiménez, they were also honoring the deceased Antonio Machado and Federico García Lorca as cofounders of modern Spanish poetry.

3. Pablo Neruda wrote his *Residencias,* his most surreal poems, during the pre–civil war years he lived in Madrid. Like his close friend Neruda, Lorca would also write his major surreal book abroad (*The Poet in New York*). Surrealism began formally as a movement with André Breton's publication of "The Surrealist Manifesto" in 1924. But if we look to the sources, the true progenitors of the surrealist movement are Arthur Rimbaud (1854–91) in his *Une saison en enfer* and *Illuminations* and Guillaume Apollinaire (1880–1918) in his *Alcools* and *Calligrames*. Unofficially, surrealism is a nineteenth-century phenomenon and as such its progenitors remain in every way primary.

4. The sudden flowering of culture in Spain may be explained by historic event and cultural circumstance, but in the end oddity and mystery prevail. In mid-nineteenth century

The astonishing poetry in Spain was commingled with major works by their Latin American counterparts: Jorge Luis Borges, Pablo Neruda, César Vallejo, and Octavio Paz. Each of these poets spent profoundly formative periods in Spain: Borges, Neruda, and Paz in their early years, and Vallejo (1892–1938) in his last years, culminating with his last volume, *Spain, Let This Cup Pass from Me* (España, aparta de mi este cáliz), consisting of poems written in Spain during the Spanish civil war.

In keeping with a rediscovery of earlier models, the secular Spanish poet Jorge Guillén became absorbed in the work of Saint John of the Cross (1542–91) and, by extension, the Bible. He found the title and model for his major work, *Canticle* (*Cántico*), in Saint John's *Spiritual Canticle* (*Cántico spiritual*), which itself is a version of the biblical Song of Songs or Canticles. For his *My Voice Because of You* (*La voz a ti debida*), Salinas chose a line from a poem by the renaissance poet Garcilaso de la Vega (1503–36), and for the second book of his love trilogy, *Love's Sermon* (*Razón de amor*), he found his title in an anonymous medieval debate poem.

The Generation of '27 contrived its name from a showy evocation of the three hundredth anniversary of the death of the baroque poet Luis de Góngora (1561–1627). The attempt to rehabilitate Góngora began with fun and fanfare. There was a pilgrimage to Sevilla, financed by Ignacio Sánchez Mejías, the literary bullfighter who was later the subject of Lorca's famous elegy *Llanto por Ignacio Sánchez Mejías* (Lament for Ignacio Sánchez Mejías). Lorca himself gave a lecture on Góngora at the Ateneo in Sevilla. This was followed by a pioneer explication of Góngora's obscure poetry by the poet-scholar Dámaso Alonso.

The cult of Góngora coincided with a rejection of all nineteenth-century models, especially those of the French Parnassians, who a few decades earlier, through Rubén Darío, an unlikely Nicaraguan import via Verlaine and the French decadents, had had such a pervasive impact on the young poets of Spain, including the early Antonio Machado. But Machado was soon to free himself consciously of the influence of the sentimental

---

America, following the emergence of the English romantics, how can one explain, in that unlikely period of imitation and postromantic mediocrity, the sudden appearance of Walt Whitman and Emily Dickinson, largely unrecognized, who were to bestow us with the major innovations of the twentieth century? The fact of a Plato and an Aristotle, a Michelangelo and a da Vinci, a William Blake and a Gerard Manley Hopkins, a Baudelaire and a Rimbaud, a Freud and an Einstein, are not inevitabilities of a historical process. There is enough wealth and patronage today for new giants of art to be out walking in the parks. Perhaps a new Sappho is busy with breakfast friends on her island and ghosts of Kafka and Borges are hiding in the Saint James Café in Buenos Aires.

Rubén.[5] He excised from his work those early poems he saw as sentimental and derivative of the Nicaraguan master in order to follow his discovery of the faces, lives, and arts of old provincial Castilla, his adopted home in the north.

Machado's own modernity contained no affection for Góngora, nor for any of the Spanish baroque poets.[6] This fact, however, never separated don Antonio from the younger emerging poets. Indeed, there was a strong and special tie between Machado of '98 and Lorca of '27 that resulted in a lifetime experience of mutual influence. At the drop of a hat at a party Federico would recite don Antonio's very long ballad, *La casa de Alvargonzález*, which served as an essential element in the development of Lorca's verse dramas, including his last published play, *La casa de Bernarda Alba*. By sad historical event, Machado's elegiac poem on the execution of Lorca in 1936 prevails as one of the century's most passionate and significant poetic utterances.

What did all this Gongorism (*gongorismo*) mean to a generation? Though different from the late symbolists, from Mallarmé and Valerie to Wallace Stevens and Eugenio Montale, Gongorism did display the extravagant imagery and metaphysical playfulness of the late European and American symbolists. In his elemental and symbolic snows, diamonds, feathers, and metals, Góngora provided startling imagery and a natural link with a modified surrealism for poets who were weary and scornful of the esthetic mistiness and sentimentality of Spanish *modernismo*. Góngora used hyperbole and hyperbatons, and extended the linguistic and musical limits of the Spanish language. All this old hard-edged sensorial poetry—with very few ideas that the followers cared about—was both hermetic and crisply extravagant, and became a perfect weapon of modernity.

Poets took from Góngora what they wanted, and no one of that remarkable generation can be accused of mannerism. Alberti composed a "Fragment of the Third Solitude" in imitation of Góngora's *Las soledades*, and Jorge Guillén wrote a tribute to don Luis in his *décima* "The Nightingale."

5. Rubén Darío did have a political, free verse side, an anger against the industrial United States, which in those days of Teddy Roosevelt had a less than admirable impact on politics and the economies of Central America.

6. I have always been surprised that Antonio Machado did not find kinship with Góngora's contemporary, Francisco de Quevedo (1580–1645), whose magnificent sonnet, beginning "Miré las murallas de la patria mía," might have found a place in his own *Campos de Castilla*, but at least the two outrageously confessional and aphoristic poets shared one figure of admiration, the fourteenth-century wisdom poet Rabbi Sem Tob, whom Quevedo had republished and Machado cites in his poems and imitates in his series of short wisdom verse.

*

Salinas developed independently, without self-conscious imitation, but Gongorism was never far from even his earliest poetry, which with wit and extravagance played tribute to the technology of rumble seats and light bulbs as the angels of the new age. Just as Apollinaire begins "Zone," his first surrealist poem, addressing the Eiffel Tower as weary of the ancient world—"Bergère ô tour Eiffel le troupeau des ponts bêles ce matin" (Shepherd O Eiffel Tower the troupe of beautiful bridges this morning)— so Salinas similarly evokes a pastoral world when he celebrates the invention of home radiators in "Radiator and Bonfire"

> Stealthy heat. Forms
> give you an unanguished
> geometry. Your body
> is parallel tubes. New
> creature, delicious
> daughter of the water, silent
> siren of winter
> who goes through radiators
> concealed in vertical loves . . .
> (*Fábula y signo*, 14)[7]

*

At other times in clear but convoluted images and ideas, he has a natural affinity with Spanish baroque complexity.[8] So we read:

> lightning rays
> of stork feathers
> so snowy they fall
> flake by flake covering
> the earth in an enormous
> white yes.
> (*My Voice*, 16)

7. The number cited is the poem number, not the page number, which holds true for citations from *My Voice* and *Letter Poems*.

8. The Spanish baroque has been reductively separated into schools of *conceptismo* (play of ideas) often associated with Francisco de Quevedo (1580–1645) and *culteranismo* (play of sounds, images, syntax, lexicon) associated with Luis de Góngora (1561–1627). The separations are of course artificial and only suggest emphasis.

Or in describing the routes of lovers who wander through the world, he writes:

A jumbled universe:
minerals in flower
sailing through the sky,
sirens and coral
in perpetual snow,
and on the sea floor
constellations
tired now, fugitives
in the great orphan night
where divers die.
                    (*My Voice*, 20)

In the early years of his formation, Salinas also likes to turn his amorous mind to such things as typewriter keys, which he calls Underwood girls, thirty nymphs whose "pure deed" is "wordless, senseless," as he places his fingers on them:

So place
your fingers firmly
and seize and hurl
the thirty eternal nymphs
against the vacuous world,
white on white.
At last they move to the pure deed,
wordless, senseless,
s, z, j, i . . .[9]

Objects and people are frequently interchangeable, for the poet's central myth is the love of reality: a love as often ironic and humorous as passionate and painful. With eros as the energy behind his vision, he moves easily from an outrageously funny and intricate poem about a light bulb (which he describes as an electric princess in a crystal palace, guarded by a hundred thousand lances of light) to the real woman he hunts for in alphabets and dictionaries and who ultimately talks to him when he is least prepared. The interest in the concrete world of technology, of radiators and movie screens, is characteristic of the radical literary isms of those

9. Salinas, in *Modern European Poetry*, ed. Willis Barnstone (New York: Bantam Books, 1980), 393.

early decades; and Salinas was particularly fond of the telephone. Indeed, his speech in early, and later, work is often easy and exact, meaningful on several levels, with the intimate, colloquial tone of a phone call, or should we say a telephone meditation.

Salinas's many talents and assimilated influences from the totality of the Spanish lyric past came together in the sequence of love poems, *La voz a ti debida*, which was published in Madrid in 1933. In linking separate, unfilled poems together as a journal of an experience, he solved some basic structural problems inherent in most collections of poetry: how to lead the reader, as in fiction or drama, from beginning to end dramatically while reinforcing, through context, each separate poem. Rainer Maria Rilke and Federico García Lorca also used a sequence of poems, *Die Sonette an Orpheus* and *Romancero gitano*, to convey recurrent motifs. The alternative, a single long poem, is very difficult to sustain. In a sequence the poems work both individually and cumulatively. By the end of *My Voice Because of You*, the persona in the series speaks with extraordinary power.

Pedro Salinas speaks with many voices, for he details love in its every complexity. Above all he celebrates the amazement of awakening to the *amada* (the lover). And when the love becomes a shadow, he returns to the enigmas of the experience with even more compelling power. The woman he kisses and hugs and lives with—in the air, horizontally, under sea foam—remains metaphorically intact throughout. She does not disappear as she turns into memory and pain.

Salinas's way is to map his love experience as extraordinary fact. He and his lover have become new people. Jorge Guillén has written, "A new *I* wants to become a new *you*. *I, you:* the relationship of all lovers."[10] In a poetry relentlessly metaphysical, Salinas maintains a distance and objectivity in his overheard confessions. We find a prosy exactitude presented through an extravagant imagination. The poet takes the simplest acts of the love experience and elevates them to convey joy and pathos. The Salinas poem has a Cervantine, oxymoronic optimism-pessimism throughout. We know, or suspect, even from the beginning, that there will be a failure. There is too much joy for it to be otherwise. No matter. He will stick with the reality of felicity, of the pink naked body, the laughter and the tenderness, the barbed words and the disappearance; for all that is real, or what he wishes to make real. Time can only alter tenses, not change the facts of the love's reality. It also has the reality of existence in the poem itself, the act of writing, which recreates, expands, and preserves the love by reliving it. Thereby he proves its persistence. The beloved is real in the

10. From the foreword, p. ix.

poem, yet events take over and her reality is a wink away from nada, from nothingness. The poems move toward darkness. By an act of will, when loss appears certain, the persona keeps inventing and reinventing the woman. Even sorrow becomes tangible proof of her existence.

> In that drowned
> reality that denies
> itself and claims
> it never was,
> that it was only my
> pretext for living.
> If you did not stick with me,
> irrefutable sorrow,
> I might agree.
> But you stay.
> Your truth assures me
> that nothing was a lie.
>   (*My Voice*, 63)

*

He remembers that when she "chose" him, he "came out of the great anonymity."

> But when you said: *you,*
> to me, yes, to me singled out,
> I was higher than stars,
> deeper than coral.
> And my joy
> began to spin, caught
> in your being, in your pulse.
> You gave me possession of myself
> when you gave your self to me.
> I lived. I live. How long?
> I know you will back out.
> When you go
>   (*My Voice*, 62)

When it is over, Salinas recognizes how the apocalypse will be:

> When you go
> I will go back to a deaf

[XXII]

world that does not distinguish
gram or drop
in weight or water.
I'll be one more—like the rest—
when you are lost.
I'll lose my name,
my age, my gestures, all
lost in me, from me.
Gone back to the immense bone heap
of those who have not died

(*My Voice*, 62)

He lives now with disappearance, memory, shadows he tries to grab, and awakens a second time, shaking. He lives with impossibility. It is not simply the loss of love—Antonio Machado tells us that love is in the absence—and Salinas recognizes ordinary separation. But it is the impossibility of leaving the circle, the trap that raises the sequence of poems from sadness to a dimension of common tragedy. Man and woman are trapped and fated to live a few seconds, invent, remember, and lose the outside as he will ultimately lose his own consciousness to senility or death. As the poems progress, the loss of so much beauty and love is expressed as a precise, unbearable fact. He relieves the "starving dream" by evocation of earlier wonder. And there is only one poem, number 61, in which he slips into total weakness, acknowledging desolation and asking that it be shared by the lover. This embarrassment, sentimentality if you will, somehow authenticates both the experience itself and the fullness and artistry of the surrounding poems. He does not willfully conceal his human frailty by self-conscious art:

Then
you would not ask
the past, skies,
forehead, letters,
what's wrong, why I suffer.
And total quiet,
with that quietness
of light and knowledge,
you would kiss me more,
desolately.
With a desolation
that beside it has not
another being, an alien

pain; that is
now alone with its pain.
Wanting to console
in a chimerical other
the great sorrow that is his.

Salinas brings to his love sequence many kinds of dexterity. Psycho-
logically, there is perhaps no modern poet—and he is above all a poet
who has neither aged nor thinned in importance—who so subtly and
rigorously uses external data, filtered and clarified in internal conscious-
ness, to give the reader an objective account of the physical and emo-
tional life of a man and woman. He is a poet of insistent intelligence, who
enjoys playing with ideas humorously, ironically, and with unimagin-
ably detailed persistence. His metaphors often extend into multiple sur-
faces and qualifications, yet clarity prevails. Indeed his elaborations are
curiously misleading, for while they appear to be ingeniously fitted to-
gether, they also have the direct flow of Molly Bloom's soliloquy, and
what at first glance appears complex is the complexity of direct, if el-
liptical, candor.

The chaos, passion, and desolation are presented in seventy linked cu-
mulatively powerful meditations on the reality of the mystical nada, of
his dying that permits her to live, and he live through the beloved.

In his pioneer volume, *La luz no usada*,[11] Julian Palley contends that the
nada, the dying from life in *La voz*, is a step in the mystical union with
the beloved, which Salinas expresses in the lexicon of Saint John of the
Cross (San Juan de la Cruz). Salinas edited the poems of San Juan, ob-
viously knew his work intimately, and Palley's interpretation is legiti-
mate. Salinas was borrowing a traditional vocabulary from Saint John to
describe the loss of self as he creates her reality in the poem. But in con-
trast to Saint John, Salinas's union is not fulfilled, not physically, passion-
ately, spiritually, nor even delusionally. In John, as in *Dark Night of the
Soul*, the loss of self occurs in the lover's embrace and oblivion. The lov-
ers, in his retelling of the biblical Song of Songs, are joined sexually in ul-
timate earthly/heavenly glory. John, speaking in the biblical voice of the
Shulamite, the woman, writes:

On my flowering breasts
which I had saved for him alone,
he slept and I caressed

11. Julian Palley, *La luz no usada* (Mexico: Stadium, 1968).

and fondled him with love,
and cedars fanned the air above.

Wind form the castle wall
while my fingers played in his hair:
its hand serenely fell
wounding my neck, and there
my senses vanished in the air.

I lay. Forgot my being,
and on my love I leaned my face.
All ceased. I left my being,
leaving my cares to fade
among the lilies far away.[12]

Unlike this scene of pastoral consummation, Salinas's nada is pain and tragic defeat, redeemed by the huge fact that in his loss of the real lover he has gained the poem and for himself the fulfilled state of being the poet he wished to be. But in the poems and in life, Salinas wishes she were truly real and his. If this were not so, there would be no pathos, no depth to the poem, and love would be a traditional pretext for devotion to the beloved, as Beatrice is in Dante and Dulcinea is in Cervantes's *Quixote*. No, at least the beloved has an earthly presence and reality, if not the illusionary one of his great passionate meditation in verse. Yet it must be said that even during the period of greatest passion, where the infatuation is true on both sides, Salinas never ventures further than the confines of a secret love, a tryst that does not, which must not, threaten his everyday family existence. After the affair has ended, and the lover marries, he cannot forgive her for not keeping the illusion of their doomed futurity.

*

Salinas photographs the mind—going down very deep, as far as the lens of language can see. At last we know who was at the bottom of the mind, so clear in the poems and now in another version, his letters. She was not as so many literary critics—even his closest colleague at Johns Hopkins, the well known historian of ideas Leo Spitzer—stated firmly, a myth, a notion of the lover, an unreality. Only his closest friend, Jorge Guillén,

12. Willis Barnstone, introduction and translation, *The Poems of Saint John of the Cross* (New York: New Directions, 1968), 39–41.

hedged, as here in the foreword (viii): "And so the woman—nameless now—becomes a you that implies some kind of mysterious Beyond." Cunningly setting off his dissenting sentiment in dashes, he suggests that for *now* we don't know who the lover is. She was Katherine Whitmore (1897–1982).

SALINAS'S LETTER POEMS

Cartas a Katherine Whitmore, 1932–1947 (Letters to Katherine Whitmore: The secret epistolary of the great poet of love, 1932–1947) was at last published in 2002, twenty years after Katherine Whitmore's death, through the efforts of many, especially his son and daughter Pedro Salinas and Solita Salinas de Marichal, who in permitting its publication also followed the wishes of their late recipient, Professor Whitmore, who detailed this wish in an elegant, candid, and moving composition written in June of 1979, which was published for the first time as an epilogue to the Eric Bou edition of Salinas's letters to her. The four hundred page book contains the most significant 151 of 354 letters written to Whitmore. The entire collection, as well as other letters, writings, documents, and photographs of Pedro Salinas, are preserved at the Houghton Library at Harvard University.

*

The poems in *La voz a ti debida* (Madrid, 1934) are a profound, personal biography of the poet and his nameless lover. In the book title, "voice" (*voz*) is the poet's voice; "you" (*ti*) his lover. But who is "you"? Because his affair is secret, unknown to his family, Pedro Salinas neither identifies the mysterious "you" nor denies critical analysis by friends who assert that the woman is his imaginary, idealized beloved as in a medieval troubadour song, Dante's *Comedia*, or Cervantes's *Quixote*. But with the legal access to the complete Salinas archives in the Houghton Library and the publication in Spanish of the selected letters, we know at last that his lover is real. Her name is Katherine Whitmore. Suddenly available is a huge documentation illuminating both poem and affair. The original poems and his signed letter comprise a second, richer biography of the poet and his lover.

The archives contain Pedro's signed personal letters to Katherine from Spain, America, and Mexico, photographs, and even telegrams sent to her aboard ship at sea. The letters have a skyful of details about his blissful and nearly tragic love. The main love epistles were born while the poems were being composed. Many envelopes with his letters include the poems he was writing or the references to ones he has composed, or are parallel letter poems that could be a first draft or later version of a specific poem in the collection. Many letter poems are simply additional love poems to Katherine. We have moved from anonymity to open biographical detail and interactive complexity. These new documents not only fill in Pedro Salinas's love story, but inform his images and philosophical meditations with a specificity of fascinating detail unfound in the poem sequence. Salinas's love poems are dominantly imagistic, with surreal baroque flourishes and sophisticated rhetorical tricks of modernity. As a late symbolist poet—together with his contemporaries Jorge Guillén, Wallace Stevens, and Eugenio Montale—Pedro Salinas uses images for their symbolic and metaphorical import, often at the expense of particularity. So a river may ingeniously evoke life, a planet a multitude, a pink flower a woman's body, a nightingale a poet's song and heart. But is it the Gándara river in Cantabria, is the planet Mars or Mercury, and what is the species of flower? What is distinctive in the nightingale? At last the places are geographical in an atlas, and the lover has a name, a name reborn in Salinas's other poetic genre, the author's epistle. Until the letters came into light, the woman in *La voz* is, like the testamental God, nameless. She is truly *Ha-shem,* signifying "the name," which is whimsically a key Hebrew name for nameless God in the Bible.

But in the poems, Katherine *cannot* have a name for family, professional, and literary concerns. Let us say, she could not be named in Pedro Salinas's world picture. Sappho, even up to the time of Salinas's death in 1951, was not recognized as a lesbian by leading ancient Greek scholars.[13] Those who knew that Pedro's lover was real were silent. In 1947 don Pedro's son Jaime spoke to me of his father's lover as we walked the night hills of Vermont. But personal knowledge was not to be public. Moreover, there were initially no letters available. When they surfaced in 1982 they were deposited in the poet's archive for twenty years before they could be seen. Hence, in *La voz* the places where Pedro and Katherine meet have no geography. The maps he frequently evokes have no coordinates. Such is the nature of Salinas's erotic poetry and also the demands of the time: a foolproof secret presentation of his great love. She is so nameless that the leading critics claimed that she was an invention.

With the emergence of the letters, we hear the other Salinas, the professor in Spain who impulsively woos his bright, almost-his-age, ABD graduate student instructor from Smith College. We discover that poems and letter poems are of equal rapture and poetic majesty. Salinas is as particular as a biologist or telegraphic operator in reporting every significant

13. See the introduction to *The Complete Poems of Sappho* by Willis Barnstone (Boston: Shambhala, 2009).

detail of the ecstatic and doomed affair. Eventually, after no hope is left for fulfillment, the years of letters disclose a new precinct of details: concealed meetings in carefully obscure sites. He wonders what town in Massachusetts can they meet where none of her or his colleagues from Smith and Wellesley will recognize them. We know the train schedules, the places in Spain or America where they rendezvous, the names of buildings, cities, people, surrounding events and atmosphere. The whole novel is there, with no less intensity and sadness, but now everything shows. The letters confirm the truth of the poet's passions and his miseries in managing them. And everything happens in pedestrian time. So does depression when things fall wholly apart.

Most of the letter poems coincide with the actual love affair in 1933 and '34 in the city of Santander in Cantabria. Through these early letters the reader sees new landscapes, sees Pedro in his room and school hallway and post office waiting rooms, waiting desperately for the next letter. Critics may translate the essence of texts for the reader. But here, where meaning is supremely secret yet essential to the force and sense of the poem, these monumentally significant letters virtually serve as a Midrashic commentary and exegesis of the original poem.

The letters are a biography of both the lover and his lover in *My Voice Because of You*. They are themselves poems contained in the typography of prose letters. Pedro asserts the poem within its prose envelope and Katherine concurs. So did William Blake and Walt Whitman when they found their free verse forms in the Hebrew Bible, which was not lineated as poetry (which is the practice today) until the 1873 *Cambridge Paragraph Bible*. They all saw the invisible poem under its prose outfit.

*

Before speaking of the significance of these letters as the other *My Voice Because of You,* I wish to note an unexpected element in the letters, which is the poet's distinctive relationship with nature. Salinas's cosmos is vast, from leaf to galaxy, but in symbolist manner the image is more often idea than its earthly image. But in the train on which Salinas traveled, nature is nature. He depicts the *paysage* sharply before lending it idea and concept. In his poems the Castilian-born Salinas rarely alludes to the lands of Castile. In his essays on the Generation of '98 poets, as a critic seeking a national identity, he poignantly evokes the severe terrain of Spain as a symbol of a new vision. But in the letters he is simply a poet responding to the landscape around him. Traveling through La Mancha, Pedro Salinas writes to Katherine, from a train, as was Machado's practice, describing what he observes. His words depict the severity of winter and a remembrance of its gold blossoming. They recall Machado's famous "A un olmo seco" (To a dry elm) in *Campos de Castilla,* with the skeletal elm tree, whose dead branches will bloom in spring and somehow return his lost Leonor. Salinas also wants the return of gold to spring leaves in his splendid evocation, but he remembers and does not anticipate. He remains imprisoned in the huge melancholy of winter, which he identifies with his own condition:

IN THE TRAIN. FROM PALENCIA TO MADRID

How gray, how brown, how austere this Castilla
I'm crossing while I write you. On the last trip
a month ago in my letter I sent the golds of poplars
bidding goodbye to leaves. Today only branches, skeletons,

and all Castilla appears peopled by erect skeletons.
What can I send you today? I must see golds inside.
If I send what encircles me it will be gray sky,
brown earth, denuded trunks, winter, Castilla.

That hurts. Since all we Castilians have gold in us
and slope into the grave huge sadness of our land.
(*Letter Poems,* 43)

My Voice Because of You (La voz a ti debida) is known as *the* great book of love poems in the Spanish language. With the publication of Salinas's letters to Katherine Whitmore, we discover another book of poems "locked in prose," to use Emily Dickinson's words, that applies to Dickinson's own letters that hold her poems locked in prose, especially the ones composed in the last decades of her life when she did not leave her house. They were her letters to the world. As for Salinas's letters, Salinas's poems "locked in prose" are different from the published poems, but not only as an addendum to understanding *My Voice Because of You.* They represent epistolary art at its finest, and more, they are Salinas's parallel voice to *My Voice,* sharing a simultaneity of creation. The letters and the poems enhance each other. It is certain that the writing in one genre deeply affects the other, whether letter precedes poem, or poem letter. If scholars wish to find the sequence of creation, the dating of the poems and letters exist.

In *My Voice* there are four essential elements in its formation: the poet, the beloved, the letters, the poems. Without the beloved no book. Without the letters to the beloved, well, who knows? Yes, a book, but profoundly different. As for the letters' survival: it was due to luck, circumstance, and the devotion of relatives and literary friends. Unlike the poems that went into his books, of which the author had copies, and that were corrected as they went through production, this sub rosa poetry was sent out, never to be seen again by its author. But it was impelled in inspiration by the same figure, Katherine of *The Voice*, and composed synchronistically with the author's same rhetorical mastery and genius.

Like biblical poetry—Song of Songs, Isaiah, Psalms, Job, and half the Hebrew Bible that until the revised editions was not lineated—until the verse is let out, the ear but not the eye recognizes the fact of its poetry. Not only Blake and Whitman found in the poetry of the Hebrew Bible their main rhetorical inspiration. Milton, Donne, Herbert, Smart, Hopkins, Dickinson, Dylan Thomas, and Eliot are a few of the poets in English whose poetry is inconceivable without its biblical sources. As for the typographical question of lineation, the poetry of Sappho and of all poets in the archaic and classical periods were not lineated. Why waste good papyrus? Moreover, the poems were never read silently but aloud and often chanted and sung. The meters were the formal structure and indicated the lines and stanzas. But the appearance of that structure as separate lines occurred in the case of Sappho in the third century BCE in Alexandria, four centuries after her death. Until the Alexandrian grammarians edited Sappho and all the earlier poets, their poetry was confined to prose. In societies that read only aloud—that had not discovered the silence of eye poetry—their cramped appearance on the page did not damage their meter and song. Even as late as the fifth century of the common era, Saint Augustine records his astonishment on noticing two fellow clergymen reading silently.[14] The ancients of Hebrew and Greek literature and scripture did not designate poetry from prose by means of visible lineation on a page.

Salinas's letter poems are fabled poetry unperceived as poetry, though both Pedro and Katherine recognized the poem in the letter. In letter 58 from Madrid, January 23, 1933, "in the margins" Pedro confirms Katherine's observation: *the letters to her are poems*:

My letters seem to you poetry.
Life!
You reconcile me with the all.
Will you always think them poems?
They may be *less,* I fear.
I'd like my poetry to serve you always.

14. See the passages on Saint Augustine in Alberto Manguel, *The History of Reading* (New York: Penguin Books, 1997).

As in the published poems, the author works his observations and elaborations into a climactic finale. The letters are rich in detail, reveal a very vulnerable author, engaging, and always extraordinarily smart and imaginative. The poet seizes on an aspect of their love. And then, as in *La voz,* with increasing intensity, develops the thought or moment into an ecstasy of elaboration, for a page or many pages, carrying us beyond the borders of ordinary being. As in the poems, this is the way of the letters or, as I prefer to call them, his selected letter poems. Salinas is a poet of culminating emotion. But his accomplished endings are not thunderous, not a drum, but a cello or flute; or, to change the metaphor, not a sword but a dart. He is the relentlessly romantic love poet, who intellectually and cunningly controls his material. Hence, when he hits us with sorrow and defeat, the effect is all the more devastating.

The poems are all telephonic, a dialogue with the lover, or a meditation she is to overhear. He is self-consciously in love, jubilantly high, perilously fearful, and ever reassuring to Katherine and self-assuring, always astonished by the loved one and by his own transformation of her. He has a multitude of ways to address her, ever searching for the new one. With this new love, he has found his total profession that will govern his life. He states very clearly in letter 113 that before he wrote *My Voice Because of You* his poems were clever, a game, an intellectual exercise. Now love has transformed his person and pen. He sees himself as a poet he believes in. As his book title exclaims, he has his voice because of her. And in the letters he constantly proclaims the name Katherine like a scriptural verse. In the poems, because of the secret nature of their relationship, Katherine must be a nameless pronoun. From the poems and letters we see that as much as Katherine is his love, she is his voice through the love poem, his literary fate, and his greatest creation.

Another quality that the letters share with the published poems is how they both move inexorably, like a detective story, through the triumphant impossible to the denouement and disaster, and a nostalgia, without remorse, to where "love invents its infinity" (*My Voice,* 70). The map of the letter poems, keeping to its own parallels, goes from furious ecstasy, critical sobriety, grief, and reluctant acceptance of loss.

The letters of early abandon and enthusiasm while *My Voice* is being composed comprise the larger part of the collection. Then, when Pedro is overheard by his wife Margarita Bonmatí while calling Katherine from his family apartment, Bonmatí throws herself into a river, but is saved at the last moment. Katherine tries to end their relationship. Heady days cede to a gradual acknowledgment of an altered relationship. Pedro tries to put the best face on it, to keep up the early dazzling freshness. He fails because the reality of a near fatality and Katherine's withdrawal cannot be dreamed away. In the fact of the failure resides the pathos, which elevates the story and the diction to its monumental darkness. So their eternal love is momentary, and in a second they are blind in the midst of light, and alone in the middle of love. Salinas chose the right line from Shelley's *Epipsychidion* to preface his volume: "Thou Wonder, and thou Beauty, and thou Terror!"

After the overheard conversation, the letters are fewer, and rather than every day they are a few times or once a year. After letter 149 in 1941 he pledges that he will not again let time fly by. But he goes to Puerto Rico to teach (1942–45) and, until 1946, he doesn't write her. In that exculpatory letter, he describes the dangers of gossiping censor agents as the reason for not communicating with her for five years. His last letter to Katherine is 151, composed in the fall of 1947.[15] By then they know the ultimate reality, as Salinas might say, not a reality he desired but had to accept. They sometimes meet, but under the strict and nervous circumstances of not being sighted together by friends or colleagues. Nevertheless, even these letters contain the clear beauty, intelligence, and sorrow of his days.

The bulk of the newly published letters punctuate the impossible beauty, the immaculate intensity, and transport in *My Voice Because of You.* There is always the reality of self-observation, followed by dismay. But we know how Salinas will survive. He tells us in the poems. Even the pain he must hang on to as a relic of love:

> I don't want you to go
> pain, last form
>   of loving . . .
>   (*My Voice*, 63)

Pedro Salinas's private correspondence sailed off on slow ships, with no presumed notion of ever reaching further than the eyes of Katherine, its total goal. Seventy years later, the letters are ours. Even more clearly than *My Voice Because of You,* they reveal Pedro Salinas as lover and recorder of that love. Curiously, what they say about the lover is intense and restricted. He praises her beautiful existence and is intent on knowing that she still loves him. But other feelings or concerns she might have seem of little importance. He keeps Katherine current about his own professional life as a major research professor, as a member of the government under his friend Salvador de Madariaga, as a founder of the International

15. In the fall of 1947 I saw and spoke to Pedro Salinas for the last time in the evenings, during a week spent at his house, visiting his son Jaime Salinas. I had attended his lecture in the summer program at Middlebury College where I was a student.

Summer University of Santander (1933–36), which was to become the Menéndez Pelayo International University at Santander, and in America as professor at Wellesley College and Johns Hopkins University. Unlike his letters to his closest friend Jorge Guillén, documented in *Correspondencia con Guillén, 1923–1951*, where the back-and-forth letters are of a friendship of thought, event, and gossip between equals, in the magnificent art letters to Katherine he is dealing with an obsession, a dream, a hope. They end there. Yes, he does give a lot in lavishing praise on her beauty, dignity, practical wisdom; he speaks his gratitude for her wondrous being, for inspiring his poems, for reading them, for praising them, and for making him an authentic poet. He describes her arms, lips, face, her extended body. Her laughter, her reserve, her absence. And finally, when communication becomes even more difficult, dangerous, and less crucial to him, he hopes for forgiveness.

Salinas cherishes each letter from his beloved. They prove their love. Perhaps if Katherine's letters were available, she would come through as a full person rather than as the poet's projection. He certainly went to immense lengths to receive her words, even using the then poorly functioning international wire services to reach her on a ship. That her letters have disappeared is a major loss. I think it probable that the poet destroyed them in order to avoid their falling into the hands of his family. Her words survive only when he cites them in his letters.

When they met in 1933 in Santander, the romantic forty-year-old married professor fell in love with one of his graduate students, six years his junior. In many ways she remained a student in his eyes even after she had become a respected Hispanist at Smith College. While very much part of the old world, Pedro Salinas has discovered his "America," the word that the seventeenth-century Metaphysical poet John Donne will, as young "Jack Donne," name his latest conquest: "my America." That was her role. His passion was real but, apart for a few professional tips about her work, she is monolithically restricted to their secret love. She was *not* an enduring friend like his poet and professorial twin Guillén, or any other of his lifelong friends from Madariaga to Dámaso Alonso. Perhaps that is the inevitable nature of such intense love. Katherine is a superreality, and in her grace and person more real than the professional and family friends, which he makes clear in his complaints about professorial and scholarly duties. It is not that he doesn't recognize her every gesture, thought, and feeling as he perceives them. Yet he understands her only as the beloved. She, the impetus for his poems, dwells in the highest realm. She is a stranger to ordinary day.

She needed to live too.

In Katherine Whitmore's succinct and generous statement, which she attached to the letters she preserved for publication after her death, she indeed authenticates her love for don Pedro, and also tells us that

> the few times I saw Pedro after his return from Puerto Rico, he seemed strange and remote. The last time was in the spring of 1951, the year in which he died. He had come to Northampton to give a lecture and we could speak a few minutes. I had always harbored the hope that he might understand why I had to break with him. So I asked him again, "Don't you understand why it had to be that way?" He looked at me with sadness and answered, "No, the truth is no. Another woman in your place would have considered herself fortunate." That dear Pedro, is undoubtedly true, but "I am not more than I." He left; I didn't know he was sick and never saw him again.[16]

*

After these observations on the letters, one can argue about old and new theory with respect to the value of information outside what is contained in the work of art. Old New Criticism proclaimed independence for a work of art, yet in his enduring *The Well-Wrought Urn* Cleanth Brooks exceeds many modern historicists in finding any significant external information to use in unraveling meaning in the poems he studies. At the other extreme, New Historicism seeks every scrap of information, usually social rather than aesthetic, to analyze the poem. What is the proper way to read a poet? There is no proper way. Moreover, we are human readers and the existence of and access to these newly published letters inevitably affects our understanding of the poems and the person. And of course, they give us the implacable presence of Katherine herself, whose reality had been routinely denied or ignored by family, friends, and distinguished critics alike. The letters are now of critical biographical significance. More, they are a masterly literary document by Pedro Salinas.

What now survives is the great voice of the lover in two major documents. The lover is Pedro Salinas and these are his compositions. There are other sequences of love poems, and probably none more significant than those contained in *The Spiritual Canticle* (*El cántico espiritual*) of the mystical poet Saint John of the Cross (San Juan de la Cruz) (1542–91), which is a restatement of the biblical Song of Songs. Saint John's contemporary and professor at the University of Salamanca, the mystical

16. Salinas, *Cartas a Katherine Whitmore* (Barcelona: Tusquets Editores, 2002), 383–84.

poet Fray Luis de León (1527–91), did two verse translations of the Song of Songs directly from "the corrupt original," that is the Hebrew, which landed the Augustinian monk for five years in the Inquisition Prison in Valladolid. Both John of the Cross and Fray Luis, like all love poets, secular or sacred, suffered their long "dark night of the soul." So did Pedro Salinas. His great love was his secret, his strength, his fulfillment, and his collapse. He wrote his Song of Songs in the twentieth century. There is an identity of speech and particularity of event, of the kiss central to both poets, and the catalogue of imagistic praise that pervades *My Voice Because of You* and the letter poems. Consider the first dialogue poem in the biblical sequence. Change the date and it is King Pedro and Shulamite princess Katherine speaking:

> Kiss me with kisses from your mouth.
> Your love is better than wine.
> Your ointments have a good fragrance!
> Your name is spread far like fragrance of oils
> poured on the body
> and so young women love you.
> Take my hand.
> We will run together.
>
> You the king took me to your rooms.
> I am happy, happy in you,
> and say your love at night is better than wine.
> It is right for me to love you.[17]

*

Or another poem in the voice of the king recounts his love in a list of sensual similes:

> You are beauty, my love,
> you are the beautiful.
> Your eyes are doves
> behind your veil.
> Your hair is a flock
> of black goats weaving

17. Willis Barnstone, "The Song of Songs," in *To Touch the Sky: Poems with Mystical, Spiritual, and Metaphysical Light* (New York: New Directions, 1998), 3.

down the hills of Gilead.
Your teeth are flocks
of lambs newly shorn
fresh from the watering
trough, perfect,
with no flaw in them.
Your lips are a thread
of scarlet and your voice
is a cloth of softness.
Your cheeks are halves
of a fresh pomegranate
cut open and gleaming
behind your veil.[18]

Among the amazing poets in Latin America and Spain in the twentieth century, the singular and most compelling lyrical utterance we have occurs in Pedro Salinas's *My Voice Because of You*. His complex song is a novel in lyrics. The professor Salinas was a literary historian of great breadth, ancient and modern. The European, the Spaniard, and, in late years, the American Salinas read all. But more than significant sources, Salinas owes his force to a fifteen-year unfolding of love and its demise in his living world. In the learned poet there is inevitably, be it the Bible, Catullus, or John of the Cross, a worldly *parenté d'esprit* with the great love utterances of the past. But it is enough to read Pedro Salinas without references to the past. The poem is perfectly self-contained. Love and its consequences remain the universal force flowing and informing each line. In them we follow his renewal of spirit and body, his transport into a relentless sublime, his being elsewhere in his pen, his heart, and the hours of actual encounters. And when he has risen from his new being to the very peak of illumination, always shaky as one is at precarious heights with nothing but summit and joy, the decent into darkness is reluctant, painful, and there comes no living oblivion providing peace. But his memory pen will not cease recording. He cannot let go. Love has made and unmade him and persists in his unmaking.

In *Love Poems by Pedro Salinas*, Salinas carries us through the deepest human adventure, a universal one. It should work in other languages because there is no expression like it; none so bright, so black, so lucid. More, it should freshen any language in which it appears. *Love Poems by Pedro Salinas* is ecstasy and fall, meditation and tragedy. The vehicle is his

18. Ibid., 9–10.

free song. It is candid, almost medical in its observation of person, act, and feeling as the drama unfolds. As a poet he has found the perfect vehicle, even perfect when it stumbles and stutters into misery. It reads like ordinary prose (there must be a rib of prose and plot whether it be Dante, Donne, or Eliot), ordinary talk and song, overheard meditation, in an extended act of unparalleled lyricism. Pedro Salinas is, for our time, the author of the Song of Songs.

Willis Barnstone
Bloomington, Indiana
July 2009

A NOTE ON THE POET (1976)

Pedro Salinas (1891–1951) was born in Madrid and, like his lifelong friend
Jorge Guillén, was a poet, a professor, and an excellent scholar and critic.
After teaching at the University of Sevilla, the Sorbonne, and at several
other European universities, he came to the United States in 1936 where
he taught at Wellesley College. The last years of his life were spent at Johns
Hopkins University. He died in Boston in 1951.

His collected poems, *Poesías completas*, with a prologue by Jorge Guillén,
appeared in Barcelona in 1971 (Barral Editores) edited by his daughter,
Soledad Salinas de Marichal. This edition includes nine volumes of po-
ems, plus some early and late poems: *Presagios*, 1923; *Seguro azar*, 1929;
Fábula y signo, 1931; *La voz a ti debida*, 1933; *Razón de amor*, 1936; *Largo la-
ment*, 1936–38 (this third book of the love trilogy appears in its entirety
only in the *Poesías completas* of 1975); *El contemplado*, 1946; *Todo más claro*,
1949; *Confianza*, 1955.

In addition, Salinas wrote prose sketches in *Víspera del gozo*, 1926; a
novel, *La bomba increíble*, 1950; a collection of short stories, *El desnudo
impecable y otras narraciones*, 1951. His collected plays were edited by Juan
Marichal in *Teatro completo*, 1957.

He did many critical editions, put the epic poem *Cantar de Mio Cid* into
modern Spanish, and wrote seven volumes of essays and literary criti-
cism: *Reality and Poet in Spanish Poetry*, 1940; *Literatura española siglo XX*,
1949; *La poesía de Rubén Darío*, 1946; *Jorge Manrique, o tradición y originali-
dad*, 1949; *El defensor*, 1948; *Ensayos de literatura hispánica*, 1958; and *La re-
sponsibilidad del escritor y otros ensayos*, 1961.

La voz a ti debida

My Voice Because of You

Tú vives siempre en tus actos.
Con la punta de tus dedos
pulsas el mundo, le arrancas
auroras, triunfos, colores,
alegrías: es tu música.
La vida es lo que tú tocas.

De tus ojos, sólo de ellos,
sale la luz que te guía
los pasos. Andas
por lo que ves. Nada más.

Y si una duda te hace
señas a diez mil kilómetros,
lo dejas todo, te arrojas
sobre proas, sobre alas,
estás ya allí; con los besos,
con los dientes la desgarras:
ya no es duda.
Tú nunca puedes dudar.

Porque has vuelto los misterios
del revés. Y tus enigmas,
lo que nunca entenderás,
son esas cosas tan claras:
la arena donde te tiendes,
la marcha de tu reló
y el tierno cuerpo rosado
que te encuentras en tu espejo
cada día al despertar,
y es el tuyo. Los prodigios
que están descifrados ya.

Y nunca te equivocaste,
más que una vez, una noche
que te encaprichó una sombra
—la única que te ha gustado—.
Una sombra parecía.
Y la quisiste abrazar.
Y era yo.

You live always in your acts.
With the tip of your fingers
you palm the world, you root out
dawns and triumphs and colors,
joys: it is your music.
Life is what you touch.

From your eyes, only from them,
comes a light that guides
your footsteps. You walk
where you see. No more.

And if a doubt alerts you
from ten thousand miles away,
you drop everything, you rush
onto foredecks, upon wings,
you are already there; with kisses,
with your teeth you rip it out:
no longer a doubt.
You can never doubt.

For you have turned mysteries
inside out. And your enigmas,
what you will never understand,
are those brightest things:
the sand where you lie down,
the ticking of your watch
and the tender pink body
that you meet in the mirror
every day in waking,
and it's yours. Wonders,
that are now deciphered.

And you were never wrong.
Only once. One night when
you fell in love with a shadow
(the only one you cared for).
It seemed a shadow.
And you wanted to hug it.
And it was me.

No, no dejéis cerradas
las puertas de la noche,
del viento, del relámpago,
la de lo nunca visto.
Que estén abiertas siempre
ellas, las conocidas.
Y todas, las incógnitas,
las que dan
a los largos caminos
por trazar, en el aire,
a las rutas que están
buscándose su paso
con voluntad oscura
y aún no lo han encontrado
en puntos cardinales.
Poned señales altas,
maravillas, luceros;
que se vea muy bien
que es aquí, que está todo
queriendo recibirla.
Porque puede venir.
Hoy o mañana, o dentro
de mil años, o el día
penúltimo del mundo.
Y todo
tiene que estar tan llano
como la larga espera.

Aunque sé que es inútil.
Que es juego mío, todo,
el esperarla así
como a soplo o a brisa,
temiendo que tropiece.
Porque cuando ella venga
desatada, implacable,
para llegar a mí,
murallas, nombres, tiempos,
se quebrarían todos,
deshechos, traspasados
irresistiblemente
por el gran vendaval
de su amor, ya presencia.

No, do not lock up
the gates of the night,
of the wind, of lightning,
what has never been seen.
Let the known ones
always remain open.
And all the unknown gates
opening
onto long roads,
stubborn, strange
tracing highways in the wind
that seek their way
with dark will
and yet find nothing,
no cardinal points.
Hang up high signs,
wonders, stars;
let it be clearly seen
that here everything
wants to receive her.
She can come.
Today or tomorrow, or in
a thousand years, or on
the penultimate day of the world.
And all
must be as smooth
as the long wait.

Though I know it is useless.
That it's all my game,
waiting for her
as for a breath or breeze,
afraid she may stumble.
For when she comes
unleashed and implacable
to reach me,
walls, names, seasons,
will come apart, pierced
irresistibly
by the huge sea gale
of her love, now a presence.

3

Sí, por detrás de las gentes
te busco.
No en tu nombre, si lo dicen,
no en tu imagen, si la pintan.
Detrás, detrás, más allá.

Por detrás de ti te busco.
No en tu espejo, no en tu letra,
ni en tu alma.
Detrás, más allá.

También detrás, más atrás
de mí te busco. No eres
lo que yo siento de ti.
No eres
lo que me está palpitando
con sangre mía en las venas,
sin ser yo.
Detrás, más allá te busco.

Por encontrarte, dejar
de vivir en ti, y en mí,
y en los otros.
Vivir ya detrás de todo,
al otro lado de todo
—por encontrarte—,
como si fuese morir.

4

¡Si me llamaras, sí,
si me llamaras!

Lo dejaría todo,
todo lo tiraría:
los precios, los catálogos,
el azul del océano en los mapas,
los días y sus noches,
los telegramas viejos
y un amor.
Tú, que no eres mi amor,
¡si me llamaras!

· 3 · Yes, behind other people
I look for you.
Not in your name if they say it,
not in your image if they paint it.
Behind, behind, beyond.

Behind you I look for you.
Not in your mirror, not in your letters,
not in your soul.
Behind, beyond.

Also behind and farther
from me I look for you. You are not
what I feel you.
You are not
what is quivering
with my blood in your veins,
without being me.
Behind, beyond I look for you.

To find you, to stop
living in you and in me
and in others.
To live finally behind it all,
on the other side of it all—
to find you—
as if one were dying.

· 4 · If you called me, yes,
if you called me!

I would drop everything,
toss it all away:
costs, catalogues,
the blue on ocean maps,
days and their nights,
the old telegrams
and a love.
You, who are not my love,
if you called me!

Y aún espero tu voz:
telescopios abajo,
desde la estrella,
por espejos, por túneles,
por los años bisiestos
puede venir. No sé por dónde.
Desde el prodigio, siempre.
Porque si tú me llamas
—¡si me llamaras, sí, si me llamaras!—
será desde un milagro,
incógnito, sin verlo.

Nunca desde los labios que te beso,
nunca
desde la voz que dice: «No te vayas.»

· 5 · Ha sido, ocurrió, es verdad.
Fue en un día, fue una fecha
que le marca tiempo al tiempo.
Fue en un lugar que yo veo.
Sus pies pisaban el suelo
este que todos pisamos.
Su traje
se parecía a esos otros
que llevan otras mujeres.
Su reló
destejía calendarios,
sin olvidarse una hora:
como cuentan los demás.
Y aquello que ella me dijo
fue en un idioma del mundo,
con gramática e historia.
Tan de verdad,
que parecía mentira.

No.
Tengo que vivirlo dentro,
me lo tengo que soñar.
Quitar el color, el número,
el aliento todo fuego,
con que me quemó al decírmelo.

And I still wait for your voice:
telescopes down below,
from a star,
through mirrors, through tunnels,
leap years
it might come. I don't know from where.
Always from wonder.
For if you call me—
if you called me, yes, if you called me!—
it will be from a miracle
unknown, not seen.

Never from your lips I kiss,
never
from your voice that says, *Don't go.*

· 5 · It was, it happened, it's true.
On a day, a calendar date
that stamps time on time.
It was in a place I see.
Her feet walked upon the floor,
the one we all walk upon.
Her dress
looked like the others
women wear.
Her watch
took the calendar apart
without missing a minute,
as they say.
And what she told me
was in a worldly tongue,
with grammar and history.
So true
it looked like a lie.

No.
I must live it inside,
and have to dream it out.
Get rid of the color, number,
the breath of pure fire
that scorched me when she said it.

[9]

Convertir todo en acaso,
en azar puro, soñándolo.
Y así, cuando se desdiga
de lo que entonces me dijo,
no me morderá el dolor
de haber perdido una dicha
que yo tuve entre mis brazos,
igual que se tiene un cuerpo.
Creeré que fue soñado.
Que aquello, tan de verdad,
no tuvo cuerpo, ni nombre.
Que pierdo
una sombra, un sueño más.

· 6 ·   Miedo. De ti. Quererte
es el más alto riesgo.
Múltiples, tú y tu vida.
Te tengo, a la de hoy;
ya la conozco, entro
por laberintos, fáciles
gracias a ti, a tu mano.
Y míos ahora, sí.
Pero tú eres
tu propio más allá,
como la luz y el mundo:
días, noches, estíos,
inviernos sucediéndose.
Fatalmente, te mudas
sin dejar de ser tú,
en tu propia mudanza,
con la fidelidad
constante del cambiar.

Di: ¿podré yo vivir
en esos otros climas,
o futuros, o luces
que estás elaborando,
como su zumo el fruto,
para mañana tuyo?
¿O seré sólo algo
que nació para un día

Turn it into an accident,
pure chance, dreaming it out.
And so when she takes back
what she told me then,
the pain won't maul me
for having lost a joy
I had in my arms—the same
as holding a body.
I will think I was dreaming.
That this thing so true
had no body or name.
That I lose a shadow, one more dream.

· 6 · Fear. Of you. Loving you
is the very highest risk.
Multiples, you and our life.
I have you, your life today;
I know it now, go inside
through labyrinths, easy
thanks to you, to your hand.
And now they are mine, yes.
But you are
your own beyond,
like light and the world:
days, nights, summers,
winters in a row.
You change inescapably
and never stop being you
in your own transformation,
with constant
fidelity to change.

Tell me, will I live
in those other climates
or futures or lights
that you are elaborating
for your tomorrow
as the fruit ripens its juice?
Or will I be only
something born for one day

tuyo (mi día eterno),
para una primavera
(en mí florida siempre),
sin poder vivir ya
cuando lleguen
sucesivas en ti,
inevitablemente,
las fuerzas y los vientos
nuevos, las otras lumbres,
que esperan ya el momento
de ser, en ti, tu vida?

· 7 · «Mañana.» La palabra
iba suelta, vacante,
ingrávida, en el aire,
tan sin alma y sin cuerpo,
tan sin color ni beso,
que la dejé pasar
por mi lado, en mi hoy.
Pero de pronto tú
dijiste: «Yo, mañana . . .»
Y todo se pobló
de carne y de banderas.
Se me precipitaban
encima las promesas
de seiscientos colores,
con vestidos de moda,
desnudas, pero todas
cargadas de caricias.
En trenes o en gacelas
me llegaban —agudas,
sones de violines—
esperanzas delgadas
de bocas virginales.
O veloces y grandes
como buques, de lejos,
como ballenas
desde mares distantes,
inmensas esperanzas
de un amor sin final.
¡Mañana! Qué palabra

yours (my eternal day),
for one spring
(flowering in me always),
and not able to live
when inevitably
in you come
new forces and winds,
other fires
now waiting for the moment
to be, in you, your life.

· 7 ·   *Tomorrow.* The word
was loose, vacant,
feathery in the wind,
so soulless and bodyless,
so missing color or kiss
that I let it slip
by me in my today.
But suddenly you
said: *Tomorrow, I . . .*
And all was peopled
with flesh and banners.
Then promises
in six hundred colors
fell on top of me.
They were elegant,
naked, but all
charged with caresses.
They came to me in trains
or on gazelles — sharp
violin sounds —
delicate hopes
of virgin mouths.
Or swift and great
like ships, far
like whales
from remote seas,
immense hopes
of an endless love.
Tomorrow! What a wholly

[13]

toda vibrante, tensa
de alma y carne rosada,
cuerda del arco donde
tú pusiste, agudísima,
arma de veinte años,
la flecha más segura
cuando dijiste: «Yo . . . »

· 8 ·   Y súbita, de pronto,
porque sí, la alegría.
Sola, porque ella quiso,
vino. Tan vertical,
tan gracia inesperada,
tan dádiva caída,
que no puedo creer
que sea para mí.
Miro a mi alrededor,
busco. ¿De quién sería?
¿Será de aquella isla
escapada del mapa,
que pasó por mi lado
vestida de muchacha,
con espumas al cuello,
traje verde y un gran
salpicar de aventuras?
¿No se le habrá caído
a un tres, a un nueve, a un cinco
de este agosto que empieza?
¿O es la que vi temblar
detrás de la esperanza,
al fondo de una voz
que me decía: «No»?

Pero no importa, ya.
Conmigo está, me arrastra.
Me arranca del dudar.
Se sonríe, posible;
toma forma de besos,
de brazos, hacia mí;
pone cara de mía.
Me iré, me iré con ella

[14]

vibrating word, tense
with soul and rose flesh,
a bowstring where
you placed the sharpest
weapon of twenty years,
a relentless arrow
when you said, *I* . . .

· 8 ·   And suddenly, at once,
because, yes, joy.
Alone—that's how she wanted
it—she came. So vertical,
such unhoped for grace,
a gift fallen from nowhere,
that I can't believe
it is for me.
I look around,
I search. Whose could it be?
Can it be that island
escaped from the map,
that passed near me
dressed like a girl,
with sea foam on her neck,
green dress and a big
sprinkling of adventures?
Won't it fall away
on a third, a ninth, a fifth
of now beginning August?
Or is it what I saw quivering
behind hope
in the depths of a voice
that was telling me, *No*?

But it doesn't matter now.
She is with me. She drags me,
tears me out of doubt.
She smiles, possible;
it takes the form of kisses,
of arms toward me;
she takes on my face.
I will go, I will go with her

[15]

a amarnos, a vivir
temblando de futuro,
a sentirla deprisa,
segundos, siglos, siempres,
nadas. Y la querré
tanto, que cuando llegue
alguien
—y no se le verá,
no se le han de sentir
los pasos— a pedírmela
(es su dueño, era suya),
ella, cuando la lleven,
dócil, a su destino,
volverá la cabeza
mirándome. Y veré
que ahora sí es mía, ya.

· 9 ·   ¿Por qué tienes nombre tú,
día, miércoles?
¿Por qué tienes nombre tú,
tiempo, otoño?
Alegría, pena, siempre
¿por qué tenéis nombre: amor?

Si tú no tuvieras nombre,
yo no sabría qué era,
ni cómo, ni cuándo. Nada.

¿Sabe el mar cómo se llama,
que es el mar? ¿Saben los vientos
sus apellidos, del Sur
y del Norte, por encima
del puro soplo que son?

Si tú no tuvieras nombre,
todo sería primero,
inicial, todo inventado
por mí,
intacto hasta el beso mío.
Gozo, amor: delicia lenta
de gozar, de amar, sin nombre.

so we can love, can live
trembling with future,
to feel her quickly,
seconds, centuries, forevers,
nothings. And I will love her
so much that when someone
comes—
and he will come unseen,
his steps will be
unheard—to ask me for her
(it is her master, she was his),
when they carry her off,
docile, to her place,
she will turn her head
looking at me. And I will see
that now yes she is mine, now.

·9·   Why do you have a name:
day, Wednesday?
Why do you have a name:
season, autumn?
Happiness, pain, always
why do you have a name: love?

If you had no name,
I would not know what it was
or how or when. Nothing.

Does the sea know its name,
that it's the sea? Do winds know
their nominations, South Wind,
North Wind, beyond
the pure blowing that they are?

If you had no name,
all would be primary,
a beginning, all invented
by me,
intact until my kiss.
Pleasure, love: slow delight
of enjoying, loving, nameless.

[17]

Nombre, ¡qué puñal clavado
en medio de un pecho cándido
que sería nuestro siempre
si no fuese por su nombre!

¡Ay!, cuántas cosas perdidas
que no se perdieron nunca.
Todas las guardabas tú.

Menudos granos de tiempo,
que un día se llevó el aire.
Alfabetos de la espuma,
que un día se llevó el mar.
Yo por perdidos los daba.

Y por perdidas las nubes
que yo quise sujetar
en el cielo
clavándolas con miradas.
Y las alegrías altas
del querer, y las angustias
de estar aún queriendo poco,
y las ansias
de querer, quererte, más.
Todo por perdido, todo
en el haber sido antes,
en el no ser nunca, ya.

Y entonces viniste tú
de lo oscuro, iluminada
de joven paciencia honda,
ligera, sin que pesara
sobre tu cintura fina,
sobre tus hombros desnudos,
el pasado que traías
tú, tan joven, para mí.
Cuando te miré a los besos
vírgenes que tú me diste,
los tiempos y las espumas,
las nubes y los amores
que perdí estaban salvados.

Name: what a dagger stuck
in the middle of a naked breast
that would be ours always
were it not for its name!

How many lost things
that were never lost!
You kept them all.

Minute seeds of time
the wind carried off one day.
Alphabets of foam
the sea carried off one day.
I gave them up for lost.

And the clouds good as lost
I wanted to subjugate
in the sky
nailing them with gazes.
And tall joys
of loving, and pangs
of still caring little,
and the hunger
to love, to love you more.
All lost, all
a thing that was before
now never to be.

And then out of darkness
you came, luminous
in young deep patience,
lightly, so the past
that brought you so young
to me would not weigh
on your slender waist,
on your naked shoulders.
When I saw you in the virgin
kisses you gave me,
the foam and seasons,
clouds and loves
I lost were saved.

[19]

Si de mí se me escaparon,
no fue para ir a morirse
en la nada.
En ti seguían viviendo.
Lo que yo llamaba olvido
eras tú.

· 11 · Ahí, detrás de la risa,
ya no se te conoce.
Vas y vienes, resbalas
por un mundo de valses
helados, cuesta abajo;
y al pasar, los caprichos,
los prontos te arrebatan
besos sin vocación,
a ti, la momentánea
cautiva de lo fácil.
«¡Qué alegre!», dicen todos.
Y es que entonces estás
queriendo ser tú otra,
pareciéndote tanto
a ti misma, que tengo
miedo a perderte, así.

Te sigo. Espero. Sé
que cuando no te miren
túneles ni luceros,
cuando se crea el mundo
que ya sabe quién eres
y diga: «Sí, ya sé»,
tú te desatarás,
con los brazos en alto,
por detrás de tu pelo,
la lazada, mirándome.
Sin ruido de cristal
se caerá por el suelo,
ingrávida careta
inútil ya, la risa.
Y al verte en el amor
que yo te tiendo siempre
como un espejo ardiendo,

If they escaped from me,
it was not to go die
in oblivion.
They were living in you.
What I called forgetting
was you.

· 11 ·   There behind laughter
no one knows you now.
You go and come, slide
through a world of frozen
waltzes, downhill;
and as you wander, whims
and impulses snatch
uninvolved kisses
from you, a momentary
captive of easiness.
How happy! they all say.
And now you want
to be another you,
resembling you so much
that I am afraid
of losing you. Like that.

I pursue you. I wait, know
when tunnels and planets
don't look at you,
when people think they
know who you are
and say: *Yes, now I know,*
and with your arms high
you will undo
the knot back of your hair
while looking at me.
With no noise of breaking glass
your laughter,
now a useless airy mask,
will topple to the floor.
And when you see yourself
in the love I always give you
like a flaming mirror,

[21]

tú reconocerás
un rostro serio, grave,
una desconocida
alta, pálida y triste,
que es mi amada. Y me quiere
por detrás de la risa.

· 12 ·   Yo no necesito tiempo
para saber cómo eres:
conocerse es el relámpago.
¿Quién te va a ti a conocer
en lo que callas, o en esas
palabras con que lo callas?
El que te busque en la vida
que estás viviendo, no sabe
más que alusiones de ti,
pretextos donde te escondes.
Ir siguiéndote hacia atrás
en lo que tú has hecho, antes,
sumar acción con sonrisa,
años con nombres, será
ir perdiéndote. Yo no.
Te conocí en la tormenta.
Te conocí, repentina,
en ese desgarramiento
brutal de tiniebla y luz,
donde se revela el fondo
que escapa al día y la noche.
Te vi, me has visto, y ahora,
desnuda ya del equívoco,
de la historia, del pasado,
tú, amazona en la centella,
palpitante de recién
llegada sin esperarte,
eres tan antigua mía,
te conozco tan de tiempo,
que en tu amor cierro los ojos,
y camino sin errar,
a ciegas, sin pedir nada

you recognize
a grave grave face
of a stranger,
tall, pallid and sad,
that is my darling. And she
loves me behind her laughter.

· 12 ·   I don't need time
to know what you're like:
knowing is lightning
Who can know you in
what you silence or in those
words you use to silence?
One who seeks you in the life
you live, knows only
allusions to you,
pretexts where you hide.
To follow you back
into what you have done before
is to tie action with smile,
years with names, and will go on
losing you. Not me.
I knew you in the storm.
I knew you suddenly
in that brutal breaking out
of gloom and light,
where the bottom is revealed
that escapes day and darkness.
I saw you, you saw me, and now
stripped naked of error,
of history, of past,
you are an Amazon in the flashing
sky, throbbing as a recent
unexpected for arrival.
You are so anciently mine,
I know you so long
that I shut my eyes in your love
and walk arrow straight,
blind, asking nothing,

a esa luz lenta y segura
con que se conocen letras
y formas y se echan cuentas
y se cree que se ve
quién eres tú, mi invisible.

· 13 ·   ¡Qué gran víspera el mundo!
No había nada hecho.
Ni materia, ni números,
ni astros, ni siglos, nada.
El carbón no era negro
ni la rosa era tierna.
Nada era nada, aún.
¡Qué inocencia creer
que fue el pasado de otros
y en otro tiempo, ya
irrevocable, siempre!
No, el pasado era nuestro:
no tenía ni nombre.
Podíamos llamarlo
a nuestro gusto: estrella,
colibrí, teorema,
en vez de así, «pasado»;
quitarle su veneno.
Un gran viento soplaba
hacia nosotros minas,
continentes, motores.
¿Minas de qué? Vacías.
Estaban aguardando
nuestro primer deseo,
para ser en seguida
de cobre, de amapolas.
Las ciudades, los puertos
flotaban sobre el mundo,
sin sitio todavía:
esperaban que tú
les dijeses: «Aquí»,
para lanzar los barcos,
las máquinas, las fiestas.
Máquinas impacientes
de sin destino, aún;

into the slow certain light
where letters
and forms are added up
and I think I see
who you are: my invisible being.

· 13 ·   What an enormous first night!
The world! Nothing was made.
No matter, no numbers,
no stars, no centuries. Nothing
Coal was not black
nor the rose tender.
Nothing was still nothing.
What innocence to believe
that the past of others
in another time was
forever irrevocable!
No, the past was ours:
it had no name.
We could call it
anything we liked: star,
humming bird, theorem
instead of *past;*
to get the poison out.
A huge wind blew
continents, mines,
motors toward us.
What kind of mines? Empty.
They were waiting for
our first desire
to fill up suddenly
with copper, with poppies.
Cities, ports
floated over the world
with no place yet:
they were waiting for
you to say, *Here,*
before spilling out ships,
machines, parties.
Impatient machines
with no purpose yet

porque harían la luz
si tú se lo mandabas,
o las noches de otoño
si las querías tú.
Los verbos, indecisos,
te miraban los ojos
como los perros fieles,
trémulos. Tu mandato
iba a marcarles ya
sus rumbos, sus acciones.
¿Subir? Se estremecía
su energía ignorante.
¿Sería ir hacia arriba
«subir»? ¿E ir hacia dónde
sería «descender»?
Con mensajes a antípodas,
a luceros, tu orden
iba a darles conciencia
súbita de su ser,
de volar o arrastrarse.
El gran mundo vacío,
sin empleo, delante
de ti estaba: su impulso
se lo darías tú.
Y junto a ti, vacante,
por nacer, anheloso,
con los ojos cerrados,
preparado ya el cuerpo
para el dolor y el beso,
con la sangre en su sitio,
yo, esperando
—ay, si no me mirabas—
a que tú me quisieses
y me dijeras: «Ya.»

· 14 ·   Para vivir no quiero
islas, palacios, torres.
¡Qué alegría más alta:
vivir en los pronombres!

for they would create light
if you ordered it
or autumn nights
if you wanted them.
Indecisive verbs
looked at your eyes
like faithful dogs
tremulous. Your command
would finally trace out
their routes, actions.
Climb up? Their ignorant
energy was quivering.
Would climbing mean
going up? And where
would *descending* be?
With messages to the poles,
to day stars, your order
made them
abruptly aware of being,
to fly or creep over the earth.
The great empty world
was inert
before you: you would give it
a push.
And next to you, hollow
from new birth, on the edge,
with my eyes shut,
preparing my body
for pain and the kiss,
with blood in place,
I was waiting—
O what if you did not see me!—
for you to want me
and to say: *Now.*

To live I don't want
islands, palaces, towers.
What steeper joy
than living in pronouns!

Quítate ya los trajes,
las señas, los retratos;
yo no te quiero así,
disfrazada de otra,
hija siempre de algo.
Te quiero pura, libre,
irreductible: tú.
Sé que cuando te llame
entre todas las gentes
del mundo,
sólo tú serás tú.
Y cuando me preguntes
quién es el que te llama,
el que te quiere suya,
enterraré los nombres,
los rótulos, la historia.
Iré rompiendo todo
lo que encima me echaron
desde antes de nacer.
Y vuelto ya al anónimo
eterno del desnudo,
de la piedra, del mundo,
te diré:
«Yo te quiero, soy yo».

· 15 ·   Deprisa, la alegría,
atropellada, loca.
Bacante disparada
del arco más casual
contra el cielo y el suelo.
La física, asustada,
tiene miedo; los trenes
se quedan más atrás
aún que los aviones
y que la luz. Es ella,
velocísima, ciega
de mirar, sin ver nada,
y querer lo que ve.
Y no quererlo ya.
Porque se desprendió
del quiero, del deseo,

Take off your clothing,
features, pictures;
I don't want you like that,
masked as another,
always a daughter of something.
I want you pure, free,
irreducible: you.
I know when I call you
among all people
in the world,
only you will be you.
And when you ask me
who is calling you,
who wants you his,
I will bury nouns,
labels, history.
I will tear apart
all that they threw on me
from before I was born.
Finally, back in the eternal
anonymity of the naked,
I will tell you:
I love you, yes, I'm the one.

· 15 ·   Happiness, quickly,
rushed, crazy.
She is drunk and shot out
casually from a bow
against the sky and earth.
Physics is astonished
and fearful: trains
stay even further
behind than airplanes
and light. It is she,
at top velocity, blind
with gazing, seeing nothing,
and worrying what she sees.
And no longer wants it.
For she has slipped out
of wanting, of desire

[29]

y ebria toda en su esencia,
no pide nada, no
va a nada, no obedece
a bocinas, a gritos,
a amenazas. Aplasta
bajo sus pies ligeros
la paciencia y el mundo.
Y lo llena de ruinas
—órdenes, tiempo, penas—
en una abolición
triunfal, total, de todo
lo que no es ella, pura
alegría, alegría
altísima, empinada
encima de sí misma.

Tan alta de esforzarse,
que ya se está cayendo,
doblada como un héroe,
sobre su hazaña inútil.
Que ya se está muriendo
consumida, deshecha
en el aire, perfecta
combustión de su ser.
Y no dejará humo,
ni cadáver, ni pena
—memoria de haber sido—.
Y nadie la sabrá,
nadie, porque ella sola
supo de sí. Y ha muerto.

· 16 ·   Todo dice que sí.
Sí del cielo, lo azul,
y sí, lo azul del mar,
mares, cielos, azules
con espumas y brisas,
júbilos monosílabos
repiten sin parar.
Un sí contesta sí
a otro sí. Grandes diálogos
repetidos se oyen

and fully drunk in essence
and asks nothing, goes
nowhere, ignores
horns, shouts,
threats. She flattens
patience in the world
with her light feet.
And she pours ruin on
order, time, sorrows,
in a total triumphant
abolition of all
that is not she: candid
joy, tallest joy
looming
on top of itself.

She strives so high
that now she is falling
doubled up like a hero
on her futile deed.
And now she is dying
consumed, undone
by the air, a perfect
combustion of her being.
And she won't leave smoke,
corpse or grief behind—
a memory of having been.
And no one will known,
no one, for she alone
found out in herself. And died.

Everything says yes.
Yes from the sky, blueness,
and yes blue from the sea,
oceans, skies, blues
in sea foam and breezes
repeat jubilant
monosyllables endlessly.
A yes answers a yes
to another yes. Great repeated
dialogues are heard

por encima del mar
de mundo a mundo: sí.
Se leen por el aire
largos síes, relámpagos
de plumas de cigüeña,
tan de nieve que caen,
copo a copo, cubriendo
la tierra de un enorme,
blanco sí. Es el gran día.
Podemos acercarnos
hoy a lo que no habla:
a la peña, al amor,
al hueso tras la frente:
son esclavos del sí.
Es la sola palabra
que hoy les concede el mundo.
Alma, pronto, a pedir,
a aprovechar la máxima
locura momentánea,
a pedir esas cosas
imposibles, pedidas,
calladas, tantas veces,
tanto tiempo, y que hoy
pediremos a gritos.
Seguros por un día
—hoy, nada más que hoy—
de que los «no» eran falsos,
apariencias, retrasos,
cortezas inocentes.
Y que estaba detrás,
despacio, madurándose,
al compás de este ansia
que lo pedía en vano,
la gran delicia: el sí.

· 17 ·　　Amor, amor, catástrofe.
¡Qué hundimiento del mundo!
Un gran horror a techos
quiebra columnas, tiempos;
los reemplaza por cielos
intemporales. Andas, ando

above the sea
from world to world: yes.
Long yeses read
in the wind, lightning rays
of stork feathers
so snowy they fall
flake by flake, covering
the earth in an enormous
white *yes*. It is the great day.
Today we can go close
to what doesn't talk:
to the cliff, to love,
the bone behind the forehead.
They are slaves of yes.
It is the only word
the world concedes to them.
Soul, quickly ask
for a maximum
momentary madness,
ask for impossible
things asked for
so long and so many times
in silence and that today
we will ask shouting!
Certain for one day,
today, only today,
that the *no's* were false,
simply appearances, delays,
innocent coverings.
And it was behind,
slowly ripening,
in measure with the hunger
of asking hopelessly
for rapture: the yes.

· 17 ·   Love, love, catastrophe.
What a foundering world!
A great horror of roofs
cracks columns and seasons;
replaces them with non-temporal
heavens. You walk, I walk

[33]

por entre escombros
de estíos y de inviernos
derrumbados. Se extinguen
las normas y los pesos.
Toda hacia atrás la vida
se va quitando siglos,
frenética, de encima;
desteje, galopando,
su curso, lento antes;
se desvive de ansia
de borrarse la historia,
de no ser más que el puro
anhelo de empezarse
otra vez. El futuro
se llama ayer. Ayer
oculto, secretísimo,
que se nos olvidó
y hay que reconquistar
con la sangre y el alma,
detrás de aquellos otros
ayeres conocidos.
¡Atrás y siempre atrás!
¡Retrocesos, en vértigo,
por dentro, hacia el mañana!
¡Que caiga todo! Ya
lo siento apenas. Vamos,
a fuerza de besar,
inventando las ruinas
del mundo, de la mano
tú y yo
por entre el gran fracaso
de la flor y del orden.
Y ya siento entre tactos,
entre abrazos, tu piel
que me entrega el retorno
al palpitar primero,
sin luz, antes del mundo,
total, sin forma, caos.

· 18 ·   ¡Qué día sin pecado!
La espuma, hora tras hora,

through the debris
of summers and collapsed
winters. Measures and weights
are wiped out. All
life spins backward,
frantically tossing off
centuries; it tears loose
galloping
down the once slow track;
crazy
to erase history,
to be no more than pure
thirst to begin
again. The future
is called yesterday. Yesterday
occult and most secret
that we forgot
and must conquer again
with blood and soul,
behind those other
known yesterdays.
Behind, always back there!
Dizzy regressions
inwardly toward tomorrow!
Let it all collapse! I
hardly care. Strong
in our kisses, let us
invent the ruins
of the world, hand in hand,
you and I
through the great failure
of flowers and order.
And now I feel your flesh,
between touching and hugs,
that sends me
back to our first vibrations:
dark, before the world began,
total, unformed, chaos.

· 18 ·   What a sinless day!
Foam, hour after hour,

[35]

infatigablemente,
fue blanca, blanca, blanca.
Inocentes materias,
los cuerpos y las rocas
—desde cenit total
mediodía absoluto—
estaban
viviendo de la luz,
y por la luz y en ella.
Aún no se conocían
la conciencia y la sombra.
Se tendía la mano
a coger una piedra,
una nube, una flor,
un ala.
Y se las alcanzaba
a todas, porque era
antes de las distancias.
El tiempo no tenía
sospechas de ser él.
Venía a nuestro lado,
sometido y elástico.
Para vivir despacio,
deprisa, le decíamos:
«Para», o «Echa a correr».
Para vivir, vivir
sin más, tú le decías:
«Vete.»
Y entonces nos dejaba
ingrávidos, flotantes
en el puro vivir
sin sucesión,
salvados de motivos,
de orígenes, de albas.
Ni volver la cabeza
ni mirar a lo lejos
aquel día supimos
tú y yo. No nos hacía
falta. Besarnos, sí.
Pero con unos labios
tan lejos de su causa,
que lo estrenaban todo,

indefatigably
white, white, white.
Bodies and rocks,
innocent matter—
all the way from zenith
absolute noon—
were
living from the light
and through the light in her.
Awareness and shadow
were still unknown.
A hand reached out
to pick up a stone,
a cloud, a flower,
a wing.
And it reached everywhere
because it came
before there were distances.
Time had no suspicion
of being itself.
It came to us
submissive and flexible.
To live slowly,
quickly, we were saying,
Stop or *Start to run.*
To live, live
and nothing else, you were saying,
Go
And so it left us
floating weightless
in pure living
with no afterward
safe from motives,
from origins and dawns.
That day, you and I
knew how
not to turn our heads
nor look far. We did not need
to. To kiss, yes.
But with lips
so far from their cause
that they saw everything new,

beso, amor, al besarse,
sin tener que pedir
perdón a nadie, a nada.

· 19 · ¡Sí, todo con exceso:
la luz, la vida, el mar!
Plural todo, plural,
luces, vidas y mares.
A subir, a ascender
de docenas a cientos,
de cientos a millar,
en una jubilosa
repetición sin fin
de tu amor, unidad.
Tablas, plumas y máquinas,
todo a multiplicar,
caricia por caricia,
abrazo por volcán.
Hay que cansar los números.
Que cuenten sin parar,
que se embriaguen contando,
y que no sepan ya
cuál de ellos será el último:
¡qué vivir sin final!
Que un gran tropel de ceros
asalte nuestras dichas
esbeltas, al pasar,
y las lleve a su cima.
Que se rompan las cifras,
sin poder calcular
ni el tiempo ni los besos.
Y al otro lado ya
de cómputos, de sinos,
entregarnos a ciegas
—¡exceso, qué penúltimo!—
a un gran fondo azaroso
que irresistiblemente
está
cantándonos a gritos
fúlgidos de futuro:

kiss, love in the flash of kissing,
and had to beg
pardon from no one, nothing.

· 19 ·   Yes, everything in excess:
light, life, the sea!
All plural, plural,
lights, lives and seas.
To climb, to ascend
from dozens to hundreds,
from hundreds to a thousand,
in a delicious
interminable repetition
of your love, a unity.
Indices, pens and machines
are just for multiplying
caress by caress,
embrace by volcano.
We must wear out the numbers.
Let them count endlessly,
get drunk counting
so they won't know
what will be last:
how to live endlessly!
Let a great flock of zeroes
assault our thin
joys, and take them, as they go,
to their peak.
Let ciphers burst
and foul the calculation
of time and kisses.
And beyond
computations, destinies,
deliver us blind—
to a vast risky depth
what a penultimate excess!—
that irresistibly
is
singing to us in fulgent
shouts of the future:

[39]

«Eso no es nada, aún.
Buscaos bien, hay más.»

· 20 ·   Extraviadamente
amantes, por el mundo.
¡Amar! ¡Qué confusión
sin par! ¡Cuántos errores!
Besar rostros en vez
de máscaras amadas.
Universo en equívocos:
minerales en flor,
bogando por el cielo,
sirenas y corales
en las nieves perpetuas,
y en el fondo del mar,
constelaciones ya
fatigadas, las tránsfugas
de la gran noche huérfana,
donde mueren los buzos.
Los dos. ¡Qué descarrío!
¿Este camino, el otro,
aquel? Los mapas, falsos,
trastornando los rumbos,
juegan a nuestra pérdida,
entre riesgos sin faro.
Los días y los besos
andan equivocados:
no acaban donde dicen.
Pero para querer
hay que embarcarse en todos
los proyectos que pasan,
sin preguntarles nada,
llenos, llenos de fe
en la equivocación
de ayer, de hoy, de mañana,
que no puede faltar.
De alegría purísima
de no atinar, de hallarnos
en umbrales, en bordes
trémulos de victoria,
sin ganas de ganar.

[40]

This is still nothing.
Look deeply in you. There's more.

· 20 ·   Wanderingly
lovers spin through the world.
To love! What unequaled
confusion! How many errors!
To kiss faces
rather than the masks we love.
A jumbled universe:
minerals in flower
sailing through the sky,
sirens and coral
in perpetual snow,
and on the sea floor
constellations
tired now, fugitives
in the great orphan night
where divers die.
The two of us. What disasters!
Where's the road? Here,
there? False maps,
juggling the routes,
gamble for our loss
among beaconless dangers.
Days and kisses
walk mixed up:
they don't end where they say.
But to love
we must ship out on all
passing projects,
asking nothing,
filled big with faith
in the mistake
of yesterday, today, tomorrow
that has to be.
What cleanest joy
of not guessing right, not finding
ourselves on doorsills, on
shaky borders of victory,
not caring to win.

Con el júbilo único
de ir viviendo una vida
inocente entre errores,
y que no quiere más
que ser, querer, quererse
en la gran altitud
de un amor que va ya
queriéndose
tan desprendidamente
de aquello que no es él,
que va ya por encima
de triunfos o derrotas,
embriagado en la pura
gloria de su acertar.

· 21 · Qué alegría, vivir
sintiéndose vivido.
Rendirse
a la gran certidumbre, oscuramente,
de que otro ser, fuera de mí, muy lejos,
me está viviendo.
Que cuando los espejos, los espías
—azogues, almas cortas—, aseguran
que estoy aquí, yo, inmóvil,
con los ojos cerrados y los labios,
negándome al amor
de la luz, de la flor y de los nombres,
la verdad trasvisible es que camino
sin mis pasos, con otros,
allá lejos, y allí
estoy besando flores, luces, hablo.
Que hay otro ser por el que miro el mundo
porque me está queriendo con sus ojos.
Que hay otra voz con la que digo cosas
no sospechadas por mi gran silencio;
y es que también me quiere con su voz.
La vida —¡qué transporte ya!—, ignorancia
de lo que son mis actos, que ella hace,
en que ella vive, doble, suya y mía.
Y cuando ella me hable
de un cielo oscuro, de un paisaje blanco,

With the unique felicity
of living a life
innocent among errors,
wanting only
to be, to love, to love each other
in the great altitude
of a love that is now
working
so detached
from what is not itself
that it looms
over triumphs or defeats,
drunk in the pure
glory of coming out right.

· 21 ·   What joy to live
feeling I am living through her.
To surrender
darkly to the great certainty
that another being, outside me, remote,
is living me.
For when mirrors, spies—
quicksilver, dwarfed souls—prove
that I am here, I motionless
with eyes shut and lips
denying me love
of light, of a flower and of names,
the transparent truth is that I walk
without my footsteps, with others,
remote, and there
I am kissing flowers, lights, I talk.
There is another voice I say things through
because she loves me with her eyes.
There is another voice I say things with,
unsuspected by my great silence;
and she also loves me with her voice.
Life—what transcendency! —ignorance
of what my acts are, and hers
in which she lives, a double, hers and mine.
And when she tells me
about a dark sky, a white landscape

recordaré
estrellas que no vi, que ella miraba,
y nieve que nevaba allá en su cielo.
Con la extraña delicia de acordarse
de haber tocado lo que no toqué
sino con esas manos que no alcanzo
a coger con las mías, tan distantes.
Y todo enajenado podrá el cuerpo
descansar, quieto, muerto ya. Morirse
en la alta confianza
de que este vivir mío no era sólo
mi vivir: era el nuestro. Y que me vive
otro ser por detrás de la no muerte.

Afán
para no separarme
de ti, por tu belleza.

Lucha
por no quedar en donde quieres tú:
aquí, en los alfabetos,
en las auroras, en los labios.

Ansia
de irse dejando atrás
anécdotas, vestidos y caricias,
de llegar,
atravesando todo
lo que en ti cambia,
a lo desnudo y a lo perdurable.

Y mientras siguen
dando vueltas y vueltas, entregándose,
engañándose,
tus rostros, tus caprichos y tus besos,
tus delicias volubles, tus contactos
rápidos con el mundo,
haber llegado yo
al centro puro, inmóvil, de ti misma.
Y verte cómo cambias

I will remember
stars I did not see, that she was looking at,
and snow that snowed up there in her sky.
With the strange thrill of remembering
how I touched what I did not touch
except with hands that I can't reach
with my distant hands.
And entirely carried away, my body
will be able to rest, quiet, dead. And die
in deep confidence
that my living was not only
my living: it was ours. And another being
lives me behind the no death.

· 22 ·   Labor
not to let your beauty
keep me apart from you.

Struggle
not to stay where you want:
here, in the alphabets,
in daybreaks, in lips.

Thirst
to slowly leave behind
anecdotes, clothing and caresses;
to reach
through all
that is changing in you
to nakedness and permanence.

And while your faces,
whims and kisses,
your mercurial delights, your quick
contacts with the world
spin round and round, giving in,
getting fooled,
to have come
to the pure unmoving center in you
and to see how you change—

—y lo llamas vivir—
en todo, en todo, sí,
menos en mí, donde te sobrevives.

· 23 · Yo no puedo darte más.
No soy más que lo que soy.

¡Ay, cómo quisiera ser
arena, sol, en estío!
Que te tendieses
descansada a descansar.
Que me dejaras
tu cuerpo al marcharte, huella
tierna, tibia, inolvidable.
Y que contigo se fuese
sobre ti, mi beso lento:
color,
desde la nuca al talón,
moreno.

¡Ay, cómo quisiera ser
vidrio, o estofa o madera
que conserva su color
aquí, su perfume aquí,
y nació a tres mil kilómetros!
Ser
la materia que te gusta,
que tocas todos los días
y que ves ya sin mirar
a tu alrededor, las cosas
—collar, frasco, seda antigua—
que cuando tú echas de menos
preguntas: «¡Ay!, ¿dónde está?»
¡Y, ay, cómo quisiera ser
una alegría entre todas,
una sola, la alegría
con que te alegraras tú!
Un amor, un amor solo:
el amor del que tú te enamorases.

you call it living—
in everything, yes in everything
except in me where you survive.

· 23 ·   I can't give you more.
I am no more than I am.

O how I would like to be
sand, sun, in summer!
So you might lie down
refreshed to relax.
So when you go you might leave me
your body as a tender
warm unforgettable imprint.
And that my slow kiss might be
upon you:
color
from nape to heels,
a darkness.

O how I would like to be
glass or quilt or wood
that keeps its color
here, its aroma here,
though born three thousand miles away.
To be
the material you like,
that you touch every day
and see without looking
around—
necklace, flask, old silk—
things that when you miss
you say: *Oh, where is that?*
And oh, how I would like to be
the one happiness of all,
the sole one, the happiness
that thrills you!
One love, a sole love:
the love you might fall in love with.

[47]

Pero
no soy más que lo que soy.

· 24 ·   Despierta. El día te llama
a tu vida: tu deber.
Y nada más que a vivir.
Arráncale ya a la noche
negadora y a la sombra
que lo celaba, ese cuerpo
por quien aguarda la luz
de puntillas, en el alba.
Ponte en pie, afirma la recta
voluntad simple de ser
pura virgen vertical.
Tómale el temple a tu cuerpo.
¿Frío, calor? Lo dirá
tu sangre contra la nieve,
de detrás de la ventana;
lo dirá
el color en tus mejillas.
Y mira al mundo. Y descansa
sin más hacer que añadir
tu perfección a otro día.
Tu tarea
es llevar tu vida en alto,
jugar con ella, lanzarla
como una voz a las nubes,
a que recoja las luces
que se nos marcharon ya.
Ese es tu sino: vivirte.
No hagas nada.
Tu obra eres tú, nada más.

· 25 ·   La luz lo malo que tiene
es que no viene de ti.
Es que viene de los soles,
de los ríos, de la oliva.
Quiero más tu oscuridad.

But
I am no more than I am.

· 24 ·   Wake up. Day calls you
to your life: your duty.
Nothing else but to live.
Root it out of the glum
night and the shadow
that covered your body
for which light waits
on tiptoe in the dawn.
Stand up, affirm the straight
simple will to be
pure vertical virgin.
Test your body's metal.
Cold, heat? Your blood
will say it against the snow,
behind the window.
The color in your cheeks
will say it.
And look at the world. Rest
doing no more than adding
your perfection to another day.
Your task
is to carry your life high,
play with it, hurl it
like a voice to the clouds
so it may retrieve the lights
already gone from us.
That is your fate: to live.
Do nothing.
Your work is you, nothing else.

· 25 ·   The trouble with light
is it doesn't come from you.
It comes from suns,
from rivers, from the olive.
I love your darkness more.

[49]

La alegría
no es nunca la misma mano
la que me la da. Hoy es una,
otra mañana, otra ayer.
Pero jamás es la tuya.
Por eso siempre te tomo
la pena, lo que me das.

Los besos los traen los hilos
del telégrafo, los roces
con noches densas,
los labios del porvenir.
Y vienen, de donde vienen.
Yo no me siento besar.

Y por eso no lo quiero,
ni se lo quiero deber
no sé a quién.
A ti debértelo todo
querría yo.
¡Qué hermoso el mundo, qué entero
si todo, besos y luces,
y gozo,
viniese sólo de ti!

¿Regalo, don, entrega?
Símbolo puro, signo
de que me quiero dar.
Qué dolor, separarme
de aquello que te entrego
y que te pertenece
sin más destino ya
que ser tuyo, de ti,
mientras que yo me quedo
en la otra orilla, solo,
todavía tan mío.
Cómo quisiera ser
eso que yo te doy
y no quien te lo da.
Cuando te digo:
«Soy tuyo, sólo tuyo»,

Happiness
is never the same hand
that gives it to me. Today it's one,
tomorrow, yesterday another.
But it is never yours.
That's why I always take sorrow
from you, what you give me.

Telegraph wires carry
kisses, touch
in dense nights,
future lips.
They come from where they come.
I don't feel the kiss.

And that's why I don't want it,
or want to owe it
to I don't know whom.
To you
I'd like to owe it all.
What a handsome world, how sound
if all kisses and light
I enjoy
came only from you!

· 26 · A present or a gift?
Pure symbol, signal
that I want to give myself.
What pain to be separate
from what I send you
and what belongs to you
with the sole destiny
of being yours, your own,
while I remain
on the other bank alone,
still mine.
How I would like to be
what I give you
and not the one who gives it.
When I tell you:
I am yours, only yours,

[51]

tengo miedo a una nube,
a una ciudad, a un número
que me pueden robar
un minuto al amor
entero a ti debido.
¡Ah!, si fuera la rosa
que te doy; la que estuvo
en riesgo de ser otra
y no para tus manos,
mientras no llegué yo.
La que no tendrá ahora
más futuro que ser
con tu rosa, mi rosa,
vivida en ti, por ti,
en su olor, en su tacto.
Hasta que tú la asciendas
sobre su deshojarse
a un recuerdo de rosa,
segura, inmarcesible,
puesta ya toda a salvo
de otro amor u otra vida
que los que vivas tú.

· 27 ·   El sueño es una larga
despedida de ti.
¡Qué gran vida contigo,
en pie, alerta en el sueño!
¡Dormir el mundo, el sol,
las hormigas, las horas,
todo, todo dormido,
en el sueño que duermo!
Menos tú, tú la única,
viva, sobrevivida,
en el sueño que sueño.

Pero sí, despedida:
voy a dejarte. Cerca,
la mañana prepara
toda su precisión
de rayos y de risas.
¡Afuera, afuera, ya,

I am afraid of a cloud,
a city, a number
that can rob me
of a minute from the full
love I owe you.
Ah if I were the rose
I give you; that was in danger
of being something else
and not for your hands,
before I came.
Since it will now have
no future but to be
my rose in your rose,
lived in you, by you,
in its smell, touch.
until you raise it
above its wilting
to become a memory of a safe
unfadeable rose
now beyond hurt
from another love or life
you might be living.

· 27 ·   Sleep is a long
going from you.
What a great life with you,
tall and sharp in dream!
Let the world sleep, the sun,
ants, hours,
all, every sleeping thing,
sleep in the dream I sleep.
Except you, unique,
alive, surviving
in the dream I dream.

But yes, a goodbye:
I will leave you. Soon
the morning prepares
its full precision
of sunrays and laughters.
Out with the dream

lo soñado, flotante,
marchando sobre el mundo,
sin poderlo pisar
porque no tiene sitio,
desesperadamente!

Te abrazo por vez última:
eso es abrir los ojos.
Ya está. Las verticales
entran a trabajar,
sin un desmayo, en reglas.
Los colores ejercen
sus oficios de azul,
de rosa, verde, todos
a la hora en punto. El mundo
va a funcionar hoy bien:
me ha matado ya el sueño.
Te siento huir, ligera,
de la aurora, exactísima,
hacia arriba, buscando
la que no se ve estrella,
el desorden celeste,
que es sólo donde cabes.
Luego, cuando despierto,
no te conozco, casi,
cuando, a mi lado, tiendes
los brazos hacia mí
diciendo: «¿Qué soñaste?»
Y te contestaría:
«No sé, se me ha olvidado»,
si no estuviera ya
tu cuerpo limpio, exacto,
ofreciéndome en labios
el gran error del día.

· 28 ·   ¡Qué cruce en tu muñeca
del tiempo contra el tiempo!
Reló, frío, enroscado,
acechador, espera
el paso de tu sangre
en el pulso. Te oprimen

floating
hovering above the world,
unable to touch it—
it has no place to be—
desperately!

I hug you for the last time.
It opens our eyes.
That's it. Verticals
come in to work
without faltering. In order.
Colors exercise
their ministries of blueness,
of pink, green, all
right on time. The world
will function well
today. It killed my dream.
I feel you flee from dawn,
easy, and travel
exactly upward, seeking
the unseen star,
celestial disorder,
the only place you can be.
Then, when I wake up,
I don't know you, almost,
when by my side you stretch
your arms to me,
saying, *What were you dreaming?*
And I would answer:
I don't know, I forgot,
if your clean exact body
were not already
offering me in lips
the great error of daylight.

· 28 ·   What circles your wrist
of time against time?
A watch, cold, coiled up,
spying, waits for
the passage of blood
in your pulse. Outside

órdenes, desde fuera:
tic tac, tic tac,
la voz, allí, en la máquina.
A tu vida infinita,
sin término, echan lazos
pueriles los segundos.
Pero tu corazón
allá lejos afirma
—sangre yendo y viniendo
en ti, con tu querer—
su ser, su ritmo, otro.
No. Los días, el tiempo,
no te serán contados
nunca en esfera blanca,
tres, cuatro, cinco, seis.
Tus perezas, tus prontos,
tu gran ardor sin cálculo,
no se pueden cifrar.
Siéntelos tú, desnuda
de reló, en la muñeca:
latido contra número.
¿Amor? ¿Vivir? Atiende
al tic tac diminuto
que hace ya veinte años
sonó por vez primera
en una carne virgen
del tacto de la luz,
para llevarle al mundo
una cuenta distinta,
única, nueva: tú.

· 29 · Cuando cierras los ojos
tus párpados son aire.
Me arrebatan:
me voy contigo, adentro.

No se ve nada, no
se oye nada. Me sobran
los ojos y los labios,
en este mundo tuyo.
Para sentirte a ti

orders crush you:
tick tick, tick tick,
the voice there in the machine.
The seconds throw puerile
lassos upon
your stopless infinite life.
But your heart
far off—
blood coming and going
in you, with your love—
affirms its being, rhythm, as something
else. No. Your days, your time,
will never be counted
on white dials
as three, four, five, six.
Your laziness, whims,
great uncalculated fervor,
can't be coded.
Feel them naked
of the watch on your wrist:
a throbbing against number.
Love? Living? Hear
the diminutive tick tick,
that twenty years ago
sounded first
in flesh virgin
to the touch of light,
to carry to the world
a distinct calculation,
singular, new: you.

· 29 ·   When you close your eyes
your eyelids are wind.
They stir me:
to go to you, inside.

Nothing is seen, nothing
is heard. Eyes and lips
are my abundance
in your world.
To feel you

no sirven
los sentidos de siempre,
usados con los otros.
Hay que esperar los nuevos.
Se anda a tu lado
sordamente, en lo oscuro,
tropezando en acasos,
en vísperas; hundiéndose
hacia arriba
con un gran peso de alas.

Cuando vuelves a abrir
los ojos yo me vuelvo
afuera, ciego ya,
tropezando también,
sin ver, tampoco, aquí.
Sin saber más vivir
ni en el otro, en el tuyo,
ni en este
mundo descolorido
en donde yo vivía.
Inútil, desvalido
entre los dos.
Yendo, viniendo
de uno a otro
cuando tú quieres,
cuando abres, cuando cierras
los párpados, los ojos.

· 30 ·   Horizontal, sí, te quiero.
Mírale la cara al cielo,
de cara. Déjate ya
de fingir un equilibrio
donde lloramos tú y yo.
Ríndete
a la gran verdad final,
a lo que has de ser conmigo,
tendida ya, paralela,
en la muerte o en el beso.
Horizontal es la noche
en el mar, gran masa trémula

[58]

the usual senses
used on others
don't work.
We must wait for new ones.
I walk at your side
deafly in darkness,
tripping over chance,
on the brink; sinking
to the top
with a great weight of wings.

When you open
your eyes I turn
to the outside, now blind,
and stumble,
unable to see a thing
here.
Not knowing how to live
in the other, in yours,
or in this discolored world
where I was living.
I am nothing
between the two.
I go, come
from one to the other
when you want me to,
when you open, when you close
your eyelids, your eyes.

· 30 · Yes, I want you horizontal.
Look at the face of the sky
in the face. Enough
worry about balance
where you and I weep.
Give yourself
to the great final truth,
of what you will be with me,
stretched out, parallel,
in death or in a kiss.
Night is horizontal
on the sea, a great shuddering mass

sobre la tierra acostada,
vencida sobre la playa.
El estar de pie, mentira:
sólo correr o tenderse.
Y lo que tú y yo queremos
y el día —ya tan cansado
de estar con su luz, derecho—
es que nos llegue, viviendo
y con temblor de morir,
en lo más alto del beso,
ese quedarse rendidos
por el amor más ingrávido,
al peso de ser de tierra,
materia, carne de vida.
En la noche y la trasnoche,
y el amor y el trasamor,
ya cambiados
en horizontes finales,
tú y yo, de nosotros mismos.

· 31 ·   Empújame, lánzame
desde ti, de tus mejillas,
como de islas de coral,
a navegar, a irme lejos
para buscarte, a buscar
fuera de ti lo que tienes,
lo que no me quieres dar.

Para quedarte tú sola,
invéntame selvas vírgenes
con árboles de metal
y azabache; yo iré a ellas
y veré que no eran más
que collares que pensabas.
Invítame a resplandores
y destellos, a lo lejos,
negros, blancos, sonriendo
de niñez. Los buscaré.
Marcharé días y días,
y al llegar adonde están,
descubriré tus sonrisas

over the sleeping earth,
vanquished on the beach.
Standing up is a lie:
only racing or lying down.
And what you and I want
and also the day—so tired
of being upright in its light—
is to be reached alive
and with a trembling of death
at the summit of our kiss,
to be exhausted
by the most unweighted love,
its weight coming from earth,
material, earth's flesh.
In the night and beyond night
and love and beyond love,
you and I
now transformed
into final horizons.

· 31 · Push me, drive me away
from you, your cheeks,
as from islands of coral,
to sail far off
to find you, to find
outside you what you have,
what you don't want to give me.
To remain alone,
invent virgin forests
with trees of metal
and jet; I will go to them
and see that they were only
necklaces in your thoughts.
Invite me to splendors
and sparkle: far,
black, white, smiling
of childhood. I'll look for them.
I'll walk days and days
and when I get there
I'll find your wide
laughters, your bright gaze.

anchas, tus miradas claras.
Eso
era lo que allá, distante,
estaba viendo brillar.

De tanto y tanto viaje
nunca esperes que te traiga
más mundos, más primaveras
que esas que tú te defiendes
contra mí. El ir y venir
a los siglos, a las minas,
a los sueños, es inútil.
De ti salgo siempre, siempre
tengo que volver a ti.

· 32 ·   Ya no puedo encontrarte
allí en esa distancia, precisa con su nombre,
donde estabas ausente.
Por venir a buscarme
la abandonaste ya. Saliste de tu ausencia,
y aún no te veo y no sé dónde estás.
En vano iría en busca tuya allí
adonde tanto fue mi pensamiento
a sorprender tu sueño, o tu risa, o tu juego.
No están ya allí, que tú te los llevaste;
te los llevaste, sí, para traérmelos,
pero andas todavía
entre el aquí, el allí. Tienes mi alma
suspensa toda sobre el gran vacío,
sin poderte besar el cuerpo cierto
que va a llegar,
escapada también tu forma ausente
que aún no llegó de la sabida ausencia
donde nos reuníamos, soñando.
Tu sola vida es un querer llegar.
En tu tránsito vives, en venir hacia mí,
no en el mar, ni en la tierra, ni en el aire,
que atraviesas ansiosa con tu cuerpo
como si viajaras.
Y yo, perdido, ciego,
no sé con qué alcanzarte, en donde estés,

That
is what way over there
I saw shining.

From so much voyage
don't expect me to bring you
more worlds, more springs
than these—your defense
against me. Going and coming
to centuries, mines,
dreams, is hopeless.
I always come out of you, always
must return to you.

I can no longer find you
there in that distance, with its precise name,
where you were missing.
Coming to find me
you abandoned it. You came out of your absence,
and yet I don't see you or know where you are.
I would go futilely to find you,
where my thought went so often
to catch your dream or your laughter or your game.
They're no longer there. You took them away,
took them away, yes, to bring them to me,
but you still wander
between here and there. You hold my soul
hanging over a great emptiness,
unable to kiss your certain body
that is about to come back;
and your missing form also ran off
and has not yet returned from the known absence
where we used to meet, dreaming.
Your only life is wanting to come.
You live in transit, in coming toward me,
but not on the sea, on the earth, in the air
which you cross anxiously with your body
as if you were traveling.
And lost, blind,
I don't know how to reach you, where you are,

si con abrir la puerta nada más,
o si con gritos; o si sólo
me sentirás, te llegará mi ansia,
en la absoluta espera inmóvil
del amor, inminencia, gozo, pánico,
sin otras alas que silencios, alas.

· 33 ·   No, no te quieren, no.
Tú sí que estás queriendo.

El amor que te sobra
se lo reparten seres
y cosas que tú miras,
que tú tocas, que nunca
tuvieron amor antes.
Cuando dices: «Me quieren
los tigres o las sombras»
es que estuviste en selvas
o en noches, paseando
tu gran ansia de amar.
No sirves para amada;
tú siempre ganarás,
queriendo, al que te quiera.
Amante, amada no.
Y lo que yo te dé,
rendido, aquí, adorándote,
tú misma te lo das:
es tu amor implacable,
sin pareja posible,
que regresa a sí mismo
a través de este cuerpo
mío, transido ya
del recuerdo sin fin,
sin olvido, por siempre,
de que sirvió una vez
para que tú pasaras
por él—aún siento el fuego—
ciega, hacia tu destino.
De que un día entre todos
llegaste
a tu amor por mi amor.

if just in opening a door
or shouting will work; or if you will only
hear, feel me, my hunger will reach you
in its absolute motionless waiting
for love, imminence, joy, panic,
with only the wings of silence, wings.

· 33 ·   No, they don't love you, no.
Yes you are loving.

The extra love you have
is shared by beings
and things you look at,
touch, that never
had love before.
When you say: *Tigers
or shadows love me,*
it means you were in forests
or nights promenading
your great thirst to love.
You don't work as a loved one;
you will always win, caring more
than one who cares for you.
A lover, not the loved one.
And what I might give you,
broken, here, adoring you,
you give yourself:
your implacable love
no possible equal,
that returns to itself
through my
body, now overwhelmed
by endless memory,
never a forgetting,
that once let you pass through it—
I still feel the fire—
blind to your destiny.
So that one select day
you came
to your love through my love.

· 34 ·   Lo que eres
me distrae de lo que dices.

Lanzas palabras veloces,
empavesadas de risas,
invitándome
a ir adonde ellas me lleven.
No te atiendo, no las sigo:
estoy mirando
los labios donde nacieron.

Miras de pronto a lo lejos.
Clavas la mirada allí,
no sé en qué, y se te dispara
a buscarlo ya tu alma
afilada de saeta.
Yo no miro adonde miras:
yo te estoy viendo mirar.

Y cuando deseas algo
no pienso en lo que tú quieres,
ni lo envidio: es lo de menos.
Lo quieres hoy, lo deseas;
mañana lo olvidarás
por una querencia nueva.
No. Te espero más allá
de los fines y los términos.
En lo que no ha de pasar
me quedo, en el puro acto
de tu deseo, queriéndote.
Y no quiero ya otra cosa
más que verte a ti querer.

· 35 ·   Los cielos son iguales.
Azules, grises, negros,
se repiten encima
del naranjo o la piedra:
nos acerca mirarlos.
Las estrellas suprimen,
de lejanas que son,
las distancias del mundo.

[66]

· 34 ·   What you are
distracts me from what you say.

You hurl fast words
sail dressed in laughter,
inviting me
to go where they take me.
I don't pay attention or trace them out:
I am looking at
the lips where they were born.

Suddenly you look far off.
You nail your glance there,
I don't know on what, and your soul
shoots out to find it,
sharpened like an arrow.
I don't look where you look:
I see your gazing.

And when you want something
I don't think of what you want,
nor am I jealous; that's the least.
You want it today, you desire it,
tomorrow you will forget
through some new love.
No. I wait for you beyond
endings and boundaries.
In what cannot happen
I hang on. In the pure act
of your desire. Wanting you.
Now I care for nothing else
but to see you wanting.

· 35 ·   Skies are the same.
Blues, grays, blacks,
repeat above
orange tree or stone:
looking at them draws us near.
Being so far away
stars rub out
the world's distances.

[67]

Si queremos juntarnos,
nunca mires delante:
todo lleno de abismos,
de fechas y de leguas.
Déjate bien flotar
sobre el mar o la hierba,
inmóvil, cara al cielo.
Te sentirás hundir
despacio, hacia lo alto,
en la vida del aire.
Y nos encontraremos
sobre las diferencias
invencibles, arenas,
rocas, años, ya solos,
nadadores celestes,
náufragos de los cielos.

Ayer te besé en los labios.
Te besé en los labios. Densos,
rojos. Fue un beso tan corto
que duró más que un relámpago,
que un milagro, más.
    El tiempo
después de dártelo
no lo quise para nada
ya, para nada
lo había querido antes.
Se empezó, se acabó en él.

Hoy estoy besando un beso;
estoy solo con mis labios.
Los pongo
no en tu boca, no, ya no
—¿adónde se me ha escapado?—.
Los pongo
en el beso que te di
ayer, en las bocas juntas
del beso que se besaron.
Y dura este beso más
que el silencio, que la luz.
Porque ya no es una carne

If we want to come close,
never look ahead:
all full of chasms,
dates and miles.
Better to float
above sea or grass,
still, face to the sky.
You will feel yourself plunge
down slowly upward
into the life of air.
And we will meet
above the unconquerable
differences, sands,
rocks, years, now alone,
celestial swimmers
shipwrecked from the heavens.

· 36 · Yesterday I kissed you on the lips.
I kissed you on the lips. Dense,
red. It was such a quick kiss
that it lasted longer than lightning,
than a miracle, longer.
                    Time
after giving you this
was nothing
to me, I had wanted it
for nothing earlier.
It began and ended in the flash.

Today I am kissing a kiss;
I am alone with my lips.
I put them
not in your mouth, no not now—
where did it get away?—
I put them
in the kiss I gave you
yesterday, in our joined mouths
of the kiss they kissed.
And this kiss lasts longer
than silence, than light.
For it is no longer flesh

ni una boca lo que beso,
que se escapa, que me huye.
No.
Te estoy besando más lejos.

· 37 ·   Me debía bastar
con lo que ya me has dado.
Y pido más, y más.
Cada belleza tuya
me parece el extremo
cumplirse de ti misma:
tú nunca podrás dar
otra cosa de ti
más perfecta. Se cierran
sin misión, ya, los ojos
a una luz, ya, sobrante.
Tal como me la diste,
la vida está completa:
tú, terminada ya.

Y de pronto se siente,
cuando ya te acababas
en asunción de ti,
que en tu mismo final,
renacida, te empiezas
otra vez. Y que el don
de esa hermosura tuya
te abre
—límpida, insospechada—
otra hermosura nueva:
parece la primera.
Porque tu entrega es
reconquista de ti,
vuelta hacia adentro, aumento.
Por eso
pedirte que me quieras
es pedir para ti;
es decirte que vivas,
que vayas
más allá todavía

or a mouth I kiss
that slips away, escapes from me.
No.
I am kissing you further away.

· 37 ·   What you have given me
should be enough.
And I ask for more, more.
Each shade of your beauty
is to me the extreme
fulfillment of yourself:
you will never be able to give
anything more perfect
from yourself. My eyes
close now, aimless,
in overflowing light.
As you gave it to me
life is complete:
you already at the end.

And suddenly I feel—
as you were entering
your own elevation from
yourself—you are reborn.
In your end you begin
again. And the gift
of your loveliness
opens—
clean, a surprise—
another beauty new
like the first.
Because your surrender is
a reconquest
turned inward, an increase.
So
to ask you to love me
is to ask it for you;
is to say to you to live,
to go
even beyond

por las minas
últimas de tu ser.
La vida que te imploro
a ti, la inagotable,
te la alumbro, al pedírtela.
Y no te acabaré
por mucho que te pida
a ti, infinita, no.
Yo sí me iré acabando,
mientras tú, generosa,
te renuevas y vives
devuelta a ti, aumentada
en tus dones sin fin.

· 38 ·　¡Qué entera cae la piedra!
Nada disiente en ella
de su destino, de su ley: el suelo.
No te expliques tu amor, ni me lo expliques;
obedecerlo basta. Cierra
los ojos, las preguntas, húndete
en tu querer, la ley anticipando
por voluntad, llenándolo de síes,
de banderas, de gozos,
ese otro hundirse que detrás aguarda,
de la muerte fatal. Mejor no amarse
mirándose en espejos complacidos,
deshaciendo
esa gran unidad en juegos vanos;
mejor no amarse
con alas, por el aire,
como las mariposas o las nubes,
flotantes. Busca pesos,
los más hondos, en ti, que ellos te arrastren
a ese gran centro donde yo te espero.
Amor total, quererse como masas.

· 39 ·　La forma de querer tú
es dejarme que te quiera.
El sí con que te me rindes

ultimate
mines of your being.
The life I implore
you to have inexhaustible,
I illuminate by asking you.
And I won't end it
however much I ask it to be
infinite. No.
I yes I will come to an end,
while you, generous,
renew yourself and live
again you, expanded
in your endless gifts.

· 38 · How totally the stone falls!
Nothing in it dissents
from its destiny, from its law: the ground.
Don't explain your love to yourself or me;
to obey it is enough. Block out
your eyes, the questions, sink
into your desire, a law anticipating
will. And fill with yeses,
flags and joys,
that other plunge waiting behind
fatal death
with yeses, banners, joys. Better not to love
looking at each other in complacent mirrors,
undoing
that great unity with doomed tricks;
better for us not to love
with wings in the atmosphere,
like butterflies or clouds,
floating. Look for weights,
the deepest in you, so they can drag you down
to the great center where I wait for you.
Total love, wanting each other like masses.

· 39 · The form of your loving
is to let me love you.
The yes with which you yield to me

es el silencio. Tus besos
son ofrecerme los labios
para que los bese yo.
Jamás palabras, abrazos,
me dirán que tú existías,
que me quisiste: jamás.
Me lo dicen hojas blancas,
mapas, augurios, teléfonos;
tú, no.
Y estoy abrazado a ti
sin preguntarte, de miedo
a que no sea verdad
que tú vives y me quieres.
Y estoy abrazado a ti
sin mirar y sin tocarte.
No vaya a ser que descubra
con preguntas, con caricias,
esa soledad inmensa
de quererte sólo yo.

· 40 ·   ¡Qué probable eres tú!
Si los ojos me dicen,
mirándote, que no,
que no eres de verdad,
las manos y los labios,
con los ojos cerrados,
recorren tiernas pruebas:
la lenta convicción
de tu ser va ascendiendo
por escala de tactos,
de bocas, carne y carne.
Si tampoco lo creo,
algo más denso ya,
más palpable, la voz
con que dices: «Te quiero»,
lucha para afirmarte
contra mi duda. Al lado
un cuerpo besa, abraza,
frenético, buscándose
su realidad aquí,
en mí, que no la creo;

[74]

is silence. Your kisses
are an offering of lips
so I can kiss them.
Never words or arms
will tell me you existed,
that you loved me: never.
Blank pages tell me,
maps, auguries, telephones;
not you.
I hug you
not asking you, out of fear
it may be untrue
that you live and want me.
I hug you
without looking and touching you.
Let there be no revelation
with questions or caressing
the immense solitude
of me alone loving you.

· 40 ·   How probable you are!
If your eyes tell me,
as I look at you, no,
that you are not real,
then hands and lips
with my eyes closed
run through delicate proofs:
the slow conviction
of your being rises
by the ladder of touch,
mouths, flesh and flesh.
If I still don't believe,
then something more solid,
palpable, the voice
with which you say: *I love you*
fights to affirm yourself
against my doubt. Next to me
a body kisses, embraces
frenetically, seeking
its reality here
in me: that I don't believe;

besa
para lograr su vida
todavía indecisa,
puro milagro, en mí.
Y lentamente vas
formándote tú misma,
naciéndote,
dentro de tu querer,
de mi querer, confusos,
como se forma el día
en la gran duda oscura.
Y agoniza la antigua
criatura dudosa
que tú dejas atrás,
inútil ser de antes,
para que surja al fin
la irrefutable tú,
desnuda Venus cierta,
entre auroras seguras,
que se gana a sí misma
su nuevo ser, queriéndome.

Perdóname por ir así buscándote
tan torpemente, dentro
de ti.
Perdóname el dolor, alguna vez.
Es que quiero sacar
de ti tu mejor tú.
Ese que no te viste y que yo veo,
nadador por tu fondo, preciosísimo.
Y cogerlo
y tenerlo yo en alto como tiene
el árbol la luz última
que le ha encontrado al sol.
Y entonces tú
en su busca vendrías, a lo alto.
Para llegar a él
subida sobre ti, como te quiero,
tocando ya tan sólo a tu pasado
con las puntas rosadas de tus pies,

it kisses
to make its still
indecisive life
a pure miracle, in me.
And slowly you go
forming yourself,
being born
inside your desire,
my desire, confused,
as day is formed
in great dark doubt.
And the former doubting
creature that you leave
behind agonizes,
a worthless being of the past,
so that the irrefutable you
can finally leap out;
the irrefutable you,
a naked certain Venus
between definite dawns,
who wins herself
her new being, loving me.

· 41 ·   Forgive me for seeking you this way
so clumsily inside
of you.
Forgive the hurting, at times.
It's that I want to take out
of you the best you.
The one you did not see and I see:
a swimmer through your delicious sea depths.
And to seize it
and hold it high
as a tree holds the last light
it finds in the sun.
And then you
in your searching would come to the top.
To arrive there
you rise over you the way I want you,
barely touching your past
with the pink tips of your feet,

[77]

en tensión todo el cuerpo, ya ascendiendo
de ti a ti misma.

Y que a mi amor entonces le conteste
la nueva criatura que tú eras.

· 42 ·   ¡Hablamos, desde cuándo?
¿Quién empezó? No sé.
Los días, mis preguntas;
oscuras, anchas, vagas
tus respuestas: las noches.
Juntándose una a otra
forman el mundo, el tiempo
para ti y para mí.
Mi preguntar hundiéndose
con la luz en la nada,
callado,
para que tú respondas
con estrellas equívocas;
luego, reciennaciéndose
con el alba, asombroso
de novedad, de ansia
de preguntar lo mismo
que preguntaba ayer,
que respondió la noche
a medias, estrellada.
Los años y la vida,
¡qué diálogo angustiado!

Y sin embargo,
por decir casi todo.
Y cuando nos separen
y ya no nos oigamos,
te diré todavía:
«¡Qué pronto!
¡Tanto que hablar, y tanto
que nos quedaba aún!»

· 43 ·   A la noche se empiezan
a encender las preguntas.

your whole body tense, now ascending
from you to you.

And then let my love be answered
in the new creature you were.

· 42 ·   How long have we been talking?
Who began it? I don't know.
My questions are the days;
your dark, broad, vague
answers, the nights.
When they join
they form the world, time,
for you and for me.
My questions drop
into the light of nothing,
hushed
so you can answer
with erroneous stars;
then, being newly born
at dawn, astonished
by newness, by hunger
of asking the same things
that you asked yesterday,
that the night answered
halfway, bursting with stars.
Years and life,
what an anguished dialogue!

Nevertheless,
almost everything is still unsaid.
And when we separate
and cannot hear each other
I will keep telling you:
"How quickly it collapsed!
We had so much to say, and so much
still left for us!"

· 43 ·   The questions start
flaming at night.

Las hay distantes, quietas,
inmensas, como astros:
preguntan desde allí
siempre
lo mismo: cómo eres.
Otras, fugaces y menudas,
querrían saber cosas
leves de ti y exactas:
medidas
de tus zapatos, nombre
de la esquina del mundo
donde me esperarías.

Tú no las puedes ver,
pero tienes el sueño
cercado todo él
por interrogaciones
mías.
Y acaso alguna vez
tú, soñando, dirás
que sí, que no, respuestas
de azar y de milagro
a preguntas que ignoras,
que no ves, que no sabes.
Porque no sabes nada;
y cuando te despiertas,
ellas se esconden, ya
invisibles, se apagan.
Y seguirás viviendo
alegre, sin saber
que en media vida tuya
estás siempre cercada
de ansias, de afán, de anhelos,
sin cesar preguntándote
eso que tú no ves
ni puedes contestar.

· 44 ·   Qué paseo de noche
con tu ausencia a mi lado!
Me acompaña el sentir
que no vienes conmigo.

Distant, quiet,
enormous like planets:
and from out there they always
ask
the same: how can you be?
Other tiny evasive ones
would like to know
gay and exact things:
your shoe
size, the name
of the street in the world
where you would wait for me.

You can't see them
but keep the dream
surrounded
by my
interrogations.
And maybe once,
you, dreaming, you will say
yes and no, random
and miraculous answers
to questions you don't know,
don't see or understand.
For you know nothing;
and when you wake up
they hide, invisible,
already extinguished.
And you will go on living
happy, not knowing
that in half your life
you are always circled
by worry, efforts, longing,
endless questions
you don't see
nor can answer.

· 44 ·   What a night walk
with your absence at my side!
My companion is the feeling
of your not coming with me.

[81]

Los espejos, el agua
se creen que voy solo;
se lo creen los ojos.
Sirenas de los cielos
aún chorreando estrellas,
tiernas muchachas lánguidas,
que salen de automóviles,
me llaman. No las oigo.
Aún tengo en el oído
tu voz, cuando me dijo:
«No te vayas.» Y ellas,
tus tres palabras últimas,
van hablando conmigo
sin cesar, me contestan
a lo que preguntó
mi vida el primer día.
Espectros, sombras, sueños,
amores de otra vez,
de mí compadecidos,
quieren venir conmigo,
van a darme la mano.
Pero notan de pronto
que yo llevo estrechada,
cálida, viva, tierna,
la forma de una mano
palpitando en la mía.
La que tú me tendiste
al decir: «No te vayas.»
Se van, se marchan ellos,
los espectros, las sombras,
atónitos de ver
que no me dejan solo.
Y entonces la alta noche,
la oscuridad, el frío,
engañados también,
me vienen a besar.
No pueden; otro beso
se interpone, en mis labios.
No se marcha de allí,
no se irá. El que me diste,

Mirrors, water
believe I go alone;
eyes believe it.
Sirens out of the sky
still spurting stars,
slender languid girls
who step out of cars
call me. I don't hear them.
I still have your voice
in my ear when you said:
Don't go. And those,
your two last words,
are talking to me
endlessly, answer
what my life asked
the first day.
Phantoms, shadows, dreams,
past loves,
pitying me,
want to come with me,
to offer a hand.
But immediately they see
I keep the form of a hand
squeezed, warm, live, tender,
palpitating in mine.
What you handed me
when you said: *Don't go.*
They go, they leave,
phantoms, shadows,
dumbfounded to see
they don't leave me alone.
And then deep night,
the darkness, cold,
also fooled,
come to kiss me.
They can't; another kiss
comes between my lips.
It does not go away,
it won't leave. The one you gave me,
looking at my eyes

mirándome a los ojos
cuando yo me marché,
diciendo: «No te vayas.»

· 45 ·   La materia no pesa.
Ni tu cuerpo ni el mío,
juntos, se sienten nunca
servidumbre, sí alas.
Los besos que me das
son siempre redenciones:
tú besas hacia arriba,
librando algo de mí,
que aún estaba sujeto
en los fondos oscuros.
Lo salvas, lo miramos
para ver cómo asciende,
volando, por tu impulso,
hacia su paraíso
donde ya nos espera.
No, tu carne no oprime
ni la tierra que pisas
ni mi cuerpo que estrechas.
Cuando me abrazas, siento
que tuve contra el pecho
un palpitar sin tacto,
cerquísima, de estrella,
que viene de otra vida.
El mundo material
nace cuando te marchas.
Y siento sobre el alma
esa opresión enorme
de sombras que dejaste,
de palabras, sin labios,
escritas en papeles.
Devuelto ya a la ley
del metal, de la roca,
de la carne. Tu forma
corporal,
tu dulce peso rosa,
es lo que me volvía
el mundo más ingrávido.

when I left,
saying: *Don't go.*

Matter has no weight.
Neither your body nor mine
joined ever feels
serfdom. Wings yes.
Kisses you give me
are always redemptions:
you kiss facing upward,
freeing something in me
that was still subject
to dark bottoms.
You save it, we see it
and see how it ascends
flying, impelled by you
into a paradise
where now it waits for us.
No, your flesh does not oppress
the earth it steps on
or my body you hold tight.
When you hug me I feel I held
a star against my chest,
throbbing, not touching,
exceedingly close, with a star
that comes from another life.
The material world
is born when you leave.
And over my soul I feel
that enormous oppression
of shadows you left,
of lipless words
written on papers.
Now returned to the law
of metal, rock,
flesh. Your corporal
form,
your soft rose weight
is what turns me into
a world of lightness.

Pero lo insoportable,
lo que me está agobiando,
llamándome a
la tierra,
sin ti que me defiendas,
es la distancia, es
el hueco de tu cuerpo.

Sí, tú nunca, tú nunca:
tu memoria es materia.

· 46 ·   Cuántas veces he estado
—espía del silencio—
esperando unas letras,
una voz. (Ya sabidas.
Yo las sabía, sí,
pero tú, sin saberlas,
tenías que decírmelas.)
Como nunca sonaban,
me las decía yo,
las pronunciaba, solo,
porque me hacían falta.
Cazaba en alfabetos
dormidos en el agua,
en diccionarios vírgenes,
desnudos y sin dueño,
esas letras intactas
que, juntándolas luego,
no me decías tú.
Un día, al fin, hablaste,
pero tan desde el alma,
tan desde lejos,
que tu voz fue una pura
sombra de voz, y yo
nunca, nunca la oí.
Porque todo yo estaba
torpemente entregado
a decirme a mí mismo
lo que yo deseaba,
lo que tú me dijiste
y no me dejé oír.

But what I can't hold up,
what pins me down,
calling me to the earth
without you to defend me,
is the distance, is
the hollow left by your body.

Yes. Never you, never you:
your memory is matter.

· 46 ·   How often I have been—
a spy of silence—
waiting for some letters,
a voice. (Already known.
I knew them, yes,
but you, unaware of them,
had to tell them to me.)
Since the sound never came
I told them to myself,
I pronounced them alone
because I missed them.
I hunted in alphabets
sleeping in the water,
in virgin dictionaries
naked and ownerless,
for those loose letters
that you might put together
and did not tell me.
One day at last you spoke
but so deeply in the soul,
so remote,
that your voice was a pure
shadow of a voice, and I
never, never heard.
For I was stupidly
given to telling myself
all I wanted to,
what you told me
and I wouldn't hear.

Imposible llamarla.
Yo no dormía. Ella
creyó que yo dormía.
Y la dejé hacer todo:
ir quitándome
poco a poco la luz
sobre los ojos.
Dominarse los pasos,
el respirar, cambiada
en querencia de sombra
que no estorbara nunca
con el bulto o el ruido.
Y marcharse despacio,
despacio, con el alma,
para dejar detrás
de la puerta, al salir,
un ser que descansara.
Para no despertarme,
a mí, que no dormía.
Y no pude llamarla.
Sentir que me quería,
quererme, entonces, era
irse con los demás,
hablar fuerte, reír,
pero lejos, segura
de que yo no la oiría.
Liberada ya, alegre,
cogiendo mariposas
de espuma, sombras verdes
de olivos, toda llena
del gozo de saberme
en los brazos aquellos
a quienes me entregó
—sin celos, para siempre,
de su ausencia—, del sueño
mío, que no dormía.
Imposible llamarla.
Su gran obra de amor
era dejarme solo.

Impossible to call her.
I did not sleep. She
thought I was sleeping.
And I let her do it all:
to go bit by bit
removing light
over my eyes;
to control footsteps,
breathing, changed
by her wish to be a shadow
that would never be in the way
with bulk and noise.
And to leave slowly,
slowly, with the soul,
so as to leave behind
the door, on going out,
someone who could rest.
So as not to wake me,
me who was not sleeping.
And I could not call her.
To feel she wanted me,
wanting me then was
for her to go with others,
to talk loud, laugh,
but in the distance, safe
from my hearing her.
So as not to wake me,
me who couldn't sleep.
And I couldn't call her.
Finally free, cheerful,
picking butterflies
of foam, green ghosts
of olive trees, filled
with the pleasure of knowing me
in those arms
to which she delivered me—
never jealous
of her absence—from my dream.
I could not sleep.
Impossible to call her.
Her great work of love
was to leave me alone.

· 48 ·   La noche es la gran duda
del mundo y de tu amor.
Necesito que el día
cada día me diga
que es el día, que es él,
que es la luz: y allí tú.
Ese enorme hundimiento
de mármoles y cañas,
ese gran despintarse
del ala y de la flor:
la noche; la amenaza
ya de una abolición
del color y de ti,
me hace temblar: ¿la nada?
¿Me quisiste una vez?
Y mientras tú te callas
y es de noche, no sé
si luz, amor existen.
Necesito el milagro
insólito: otro día
y tu voz, confirmándome
el prodigio de siempre.
Y aunque te calles tú,
en la enorme distancia,
la aurora, por lo menos,
la aurora, sí. La luz
que ella me traiga hoy
será el gran sí del mundo
al amor que te tengo.

· 49 ·   Tú no puedes quererme:
estás alta, ¡qué arriba!
Y para consolarme
me envías sombras, copias,
retratos, simulacros,
todos tan parecidos
como si fueses tú.
Entre figuraciones
vivo, de ti, sin ti.
Me quieren,
me acompañan. Nos vamos

· 48 · Night is the great doubt
of the world and of your love.
I need that day
each day tell me
it is day, that it is
day and light: and you there.
The gigantic sinking
of marble and reeds,
the great blotting out
of wing and flower:
the night; already the threat
of the abolition
of color and of you
makes me tremble. Is there nothing?
Did you once love me?
And while you are silent
and it is night, I don't know
if light and love exist.
I need the uncustomary
miracle: another day
and your voice confirming
the usual marvel.
And though you are silent,
in the enormous distance
at least the dawn,
yes, the dawn. The light
she might bring me today
will be the great yes of the world
to the love I have for you.

· 49 · You cannot love me:
you are loftily high!
And to console me
you send shadows, copies,
pictures, simulacra,
all so alike
as if they were you.
I live between live images
of you, without you.
They like me,
go with me. We go

por los claustros del agua,
por los hielos flotantes,
por la pampa, o a cines
minúsculos y hondos.
Siempre hablando de ti.
Me dicen:
«No somos ella, pero
¡si tú vieras qué iguales!»
Tus espectros, qué brazos
largos, qué labios duros
tienen: sí, como tú.
Por fingir que me quieres,
me abrazan y me besan.
Sus voces tiernas dicen
que tú abrazas, que tú
besas así. Yo vivo
de sombras, entre sombras
de carne tibia, bella,
con tus ojos, tu cuerpo,
tus besos, sí, con todo
lo tuyo menos tú.
Con criaturas falsas,
divinas, interpuestas
para que ese gran beso
que no podemos darnos
me lo den, se lo dé.

· 50 · Se te está viendo la otra.
Se parece a ti:
los pasos, el mismo ceño,
los mismos tacones altos
todos manchados de estrellas.
Cuando vayáis por la calle
juntas, las dos,
¡qué difícil el saber
quién eres, quién no eres tú!
Tan iguales ya, que sea
imposible vivir más
así, siendo tan iguales.
Y como tú eres la frágil,
la apenas siendo, tiernísima,

[92]

through cloisters of water,
through floating icebergs,
through the pampas or to deep
and diminutive movies.
Always talking about you.
They tell me:
We are not she, but
if you saw how alike we are!
Your phantoms, what long
arms, hard lips
they have. yes, like you.
To act as if you cared,
they hug me and kiss me.
Their tender voices say
that you hug and kiss
like this. I live
on shadows, among shadows
of warm beautiful flesh,
with your eyes, your body,
your kisses, yes, with all
of you except you.
With false creatures
mediating divinely
so that the great kiss
we cannot give each other
they give me, I give them.

· 50 ·   The other one shows through you.
She looks like you:
her steps, the same frown,
same high heels
all stained with stars.
When the two of you go
down the street
how tricky it is to know
who you are, who is not you!
So much alike that it's
impossible to go on living
like that, so alike.
And since you are fragile,
scarcely existing, tender,

[93]

tú tienes que ser la muerta.
Tú dejarás que te mate,
que siga viviendo ella,
embustera, falsa tú,
pero tan igual a ti
que nadie se acordará
sino yo de lo que eras.
Y vendrá un día
—porque vendrá, sí, vendrá—
en que al mirarme a los ojos
tú veas
que pienso en ella y la quiero:
tú veas que no eres tú.

· 51 · No, no puedo creer
que seas para mí,
si te acercas, y llegas
y me dices: «Te quiero.»
¿Amar tú? ¿Tú, belleza
que vives por encima,
como estrella o abril,
del gran sino de amar,
en la gran altitud,
donde no se contesta?
¿Me sonríe a mí el sol,
o la noche, o la ola?
¿Rueda para mí el mundo
jugándose estaciones,
naranjas, hojas secas?
No sonríen, no ruedan
para mí, para otros.
Bellezas suficientes,
reclusas, nada quieren,
en su altura, implacables.
Indiferentemente,
salen, se pintan, huyen,
dejándose detrás
afanosos tropeles
de anhelos y palabras.
Se dejan amar, sí,
pero nunca responden

[94]

you must be the dead one.
You will let her kill you
so she may go on living,
an imposter, a fake you
but so alike
that no one but me
will remember what you were.
And one day—
it will come, yes, it will come—
when you look me in the eyes
you see
that I think of her and love her:
you see that you are not you.

· 51 ·   No, I can't believe
you are for me,
if you come near, if you come
and tell me: "I want you."
Can you love? You? Beauty
living above,
like a star or April,
in the immense fate of loving,
in that immense altitude
where no one answers?
Will the sun or night
or a wave smile at me?
Does the world spin for me,
playing its seasons,
oranges, dry leaves?
They don't smile, don't spin
for me or for others.
Self-contained and cloistered
beauties want nothing
in their inexorable height.
Indifferent,
they go out, put on makeup,
fly off, leaving behind
eager troupes
of longing and words.
They let themselves be loved, yes,
but never respond

queriendo.
Florecer, deshojarse,
olas, hierbas, mañanas:
pastos para corderos,
juegos de niños y
silencios absolutos.
Mas para nadie amor.
Nosotros, sí, nosotros,
amando, los amantes.

· 52 ·   Distánciamela, espejo;
trastorna su tamaño.
A ella, que llena el mundo,
hazla menuda, mínima.
Que quepa en monosílabos,
en unos ojos;
que la puedas tener
a ella, desmesurada,
gacela, ya sujeta,
infantil, en tu marco.
Quítale esa delicia
del ardor y del bulto,
que no la sientan ya
las últimas balanzas;
déjala fría, lisa,
enterrada en tu azogue.
Desvía
su mirada; que no
me vea, que se crea
que está sola.
Que yo sepa, por fin,
cómo es cuando esté sola.
Entrégame tú de ella
lo que no me dio nunca.

Aunque así
—¡qué verdad revelada!—,
aunque así, me la quites.

with desire.
They flower, their leaves drop,
waves, grass, mornings:
pasture for lambs,
children's games
and absolute silences.
But love for no one.
We, yes, we
loving, the lovers.

· 52 ·   Mirror, get me away from her.
Transform her size.
Make her—who fills the world—
make her minute, minimal.
Let her fit in monosyllables,
in eyes
so you can hold her,
that immeasurable
gazelle, captive now,
childlike in your frame.
Remove the ecstasy
of ardor and volume
so that the last scales
won't feel her.
Leave her cold, smooth,
buried in your quicksilver.
Deflect
her gaze; for her
not to see me, for her to think
she is alone.
That I may know finally
how she is when she is alone.
Glass, give me from her
what she never gave me.

Though in this way—
what transparent truth!—
though in this way, you take her from me.

· 53 · Entre tu verdad más honda
y yo
me pones siempre tus besos.
La presiento, cerca ya,
la deseo, no la alcanzo;
cuando estoy más cerca de ella
me cierras el paso tú,
te me ofreces en los labios.
Y ya no voy más allá.
Triunfas. Olvido, besando,
tu secreto encastillado.
Y me truecas el afán
de seguir más hacia ti,
en deseo
de que no me dejes ir
y me beses.
Ten cuidado.
Te vas a vender, así.
Porque un día el beso tuyo,
de tan lejos, de tan hondo
te va a nacer,
que lo que estás escondiendo
detrás de él
te salte todo a los labios.
Y lo que tú me negabas
—alma delgada y esquiva—
se me entregue, me lo des
sin querer
donde querías negármelo.

· 54 · La frente es más segura.
Los labios ceden, rinden
su forma al otro labio
que los viene a besar.
Nos creemos
que allí se aprieta el mundo,
que se cierran
el final y el principio:
engañan sin querer.
Pero la frente es dura;
por detrás de la carne

· 53 · Between your deepest truth
and me
you always place your kisses.
I sense it near,
desire it, don't reach it;
when I am closer to it
you block my way,
you offer yourself in your lips.
And I don't go any further.
You triumph. Kissing, I forget
your secret shut in a castle.
And you convert my longing
to go further toward you
in a desire
that you won't let me escape from
and you kiss me.
Be careful.
That's a way of selling yourself.
One day your kiss
will emerge
from so far, so deep,
that what you conceal
behind it
will spring fully into your lips.
And what you denied me—
thin and elusive soul—
will reach me, you giving it,
not wanting to,
where you wanted to deny me it.

· 54 · The forehead is safer.
Lips give in, give up
their form to the other lip
that just kissed them.
We believe
the world is squeezed in there,
closing off
the end and beginning:
they fool us, not meaning to.
But the forehead is hardness
behind the flesh,

[99]

está, rígida, eterna,
la respuesta inflexible,
monosílaba, el hueso.
Se maduran los mundos
tras de su fortaleza.
Nada se puede ver
ni tocar. Sonrosada
o morena, la piel
disfraza levemente
la defensa absoluta
del ser último. Besos
me entregas y dulzuras
esenciales del mundo,
en su fruto redondo,
aquí en los labios. Pero
cuando toco tu frente
con mi frente, te siento
la amada más distante,
la más última, esa
que ha de durar, secreta,
cuando pasen los labios,
sus besos. Salvación
—fría, dura en la tierra—
del gran contacto ardiente
que esta noche consume

· 55 ·   No preguntarte me salva.
Si llegase a preguntar
antes de decir tú nada,
¡qué claro estaría todo,
todo qué acabado ya!
Sería cambiar tus brazos,
tus auroras, indecisas
de hacia quién,
sería cambiar la duda
donde vives, donde vivo
como en un gran mundo a oscuras,
por una moneda fría
y clara: lo que es verdad.
Te marcharías, entonces.
Donde está tu cuerpo ahora,

[100]

stiff, eternal, an inflexible answer,
a monosyllable: the bone.
Worlds ripen
behind that fortress.
Nothing can be seen
or touched. Rosy
or dark skin
lightly masks
the absolute defense
of ultimate being. You
surrender kisses and essential
sweetness in the world
in a round fruit,
here on lips. But
when I touch your forehead
with my forehead, I feel you
the most distant lover,
the ultimate one
who will last secretly
when lips
and kisses pass. Salvation,
cold, hard on the earth,
of the great ardent contact
that this night burns.

· 55 · Not asking you saves me.
If I did ask
before you said anything,
how clear it would all be,
all over with now!
It would be to change your arms,
your dawns, indecisive
where they are going.
It would be to change the doubt
where you live, where I live
as in a great unlit world,
for a cold bright
coin: the truth.
You would go off then.
Where your body now is,

vacilante, todo trémulo
de besarme o no, estaría
la certidumbre: tu ausencia
sin labios. Y donde está
ahora la angustia, el tormento,
cielos negros, estrellados
de puede ser, de quizás,
no habría más que ella sola.
Mi única amante ya siempre,
y yo a tu lado, sin ti.
Yo solo con la verdad.

Me estoy labrando tu sombra.
La tengo ya sin los labios,
rojos y duros: ardían.
Te los habría besado
aún mucho más.

Luego te paro los brazos,
rápidos, largos, nerviosos.
Me ofrecían el camino
para que yo te estrechara.

Te arranco el color, el bulto.
Te mato el paso. Venías
derecha a mí. Lo que más
pena me ha dado, al callártela,
es tu voz. Densa, tan cálida,
más palpable que tu cuerpo.
Pero ya iba a traicionarnos.

Así
mi amor está libre, suelto,
con tu sombra descarnada.
Y puedo vivir en ti
sin temor
a lo que yo más deseo,
a tu beso, a tus abrazos.
Estar ya siempre pensando
en los labios, en la voz,
en el cuerpo,

vacillating, all trembling
about kissing me or not;
it would be certainty: your lipless
absence. And where now
are anguish, torment,
skies black with possible
stars, with perhaps.
It would be only she alone.
My only lover now always,
and I beside you without you.
I alone with the truth.

· 56 ·   I am forming your shadow.
Now I have it without those red
and hard lips: they were burning.
I would have kissed them
even more.

Then I parry your quick,
long nervous arms.
They offered me the road
so I could confine you on it.

I pull out color, mass.
I kill off your step. You were coming
right to me. What hurt me most
when I silenced it in you
is your voice. Rich, so warm,
more palpable than your body.
But it was set to betray us.

So
my love is free, loose,
with your bodiless shadow.
And I can live in you
with no fear
of what I most desire,
of your kiss, your arms.
To be always brooding
on your lips, on your voice,
on your body

que yo mismo te arranqué
para poder, ya sin ellos,
quererte.
¡Yo, que los quería tanto!
Y estrechar sin fin, sin pena
—mientras se va inasidera,
con mi gran amor detrás,
la carne por su camino—
tu solo cuerpo posible:
tu dulce cuerpo pensado.

· 57 ·   Dime, ¿por qué ese afán
de hacerte la posible,
si sabes que tú eres
la que no serás nunca?
Tú a mi lado, en tu carne,
en tu cuerpo, eres sólo
el gran deseo inútil
de estar aquí a mi lado
en tu cuerpo, en tu carne.
En todo lo que haces,
verdadero, visible,
no se consuma nada,
ni se realiza, no.
Lo que tú haces no es más
que lo que tú querrías
hacer mientras lo haces.
Las palabras, las manos
que me entregas, las beso
por esa voluntad
tuya e irrealizable
de dármelas, al dármelas.
Y cuanto más te acercas
contra mí y más te estrechas
contra el no indestructible
y negro, más se ensanchan
de querer abolirlas,
de afán de que no existan,
las distancias sin fondo
que quieres ignorar
abrazándome. Y siento

that I stripped from you
so now without them
I can love you.
And confined endlessly, with no pain—
with my great love behind
your flesh not held back
and on its road—
to your only possible body,
your sweet body in my mind.

· 57 · Tell me, why that thirst
to make you possible
when you know you are
one who will never be?
You at my side, in your flesh,
in your body, are only
the great crazy wish
to be here at my side
in your body, in your flesh.
In everything you do
true, visible,
nothing is flaming
or accomplished. No.
What you do is just
what you want to do,
doing it.
The words, hands
you let me have, I kiss
through your own unrealizable will
of giving as you give.
And the closer you come
to me and deeper you press
against the indestructible and black
no, the vaster
is your thirst to abolish them,
to make them not be
the hollow distances
you like to ignore
when you hug me. I feel
your living with me

que tu vivir conmigo
es signo puro, seña,
en besos, en presencias
de lo imposible, de
tu querer vivir
conmigo, mía, siempre.

· 58 ·   Te busqué por la duda:
no te encontraba nunca.

Me fui a tu encuentro
por el dolor.
Tú no venías por allí.

Me metí en lo más hondo
por ver si, al fin, estabas.
Por la angustia,
desgarradora, hiriéndome.
Tú no surgías nunca de la herida.
Y nadie me hizo señas
—un jardín o tus labios,
con árboles, con besos—;
nadie me dijo
—por eso te perdí—
que tú ibas por las últimas
terrazas de la risa,
del gozo, de lo cierto.
Que a ti se te encontraba
en las cimas del beso
sin duda y sin mañana.
En el vértice puro
de la alegría alta,
multiplicando júbilos
por júbilos, por risas,
por placeres.
Apuntando en el aire
las cifras fabulosas,
sin peso, de tu dicha.

is pure sign, signal
in kisses, in presences,
of the impossible,
of wishing to live
with me, mine, always.

· 58 ·   I looked for you through doubt:
I never found you.

I went to meet you
through pain.
You didn't come that way.

I went down to the very bottom
to see if, finally, you were there.
Through anguish
ripping, wounding me.
You never came out of the incision.
And no one gave me a hint—
a garden or your lips
with trees, with kisses;
no one told me—
that's why I lost you—
that you were moving through the last
terraces of laughter,
of pleasure, of what is sure.
That you were really
on the peaks of a kiss,
unalarmed, with no future.
On the steep vertex
of tall joy,
multiplying ecstasy
by ecstasy, by laughter
by pleasures.
That you were jotting down
fabulous airy ciphers on the air
of your happiness.

A ti sólo se llega
por ti. Te espero.

Yo sí que sé dónde estoy,
mi ciudad, la calle, el nombre
por el que todos me llaman.
Pero no sé dónde estuve
contigo.
Allí me llevaste tú.

¿Cómo
iba a aprender el camino
si yo no miraba a nada
más que a ti,
si el camino era tu andar,
y el final
fue cuando tú te paraste?
¿Qué más podía haber ya
que tú ofrecida, mirándome?

Pero ahora,
¡qué desterrado, qué ausente
es estar donde uno está!
Espero, pasan los trenes,
los azares, las miradas.
Me llevarían adonde
nunca he estado. Pero yo
no quiero los cielos nuevos.
Yo quiero estar donde estuve.
Contigo, volver.
¡Qué novedad tan inmensa
eso, volver otra vez,
repetir lo nunca igual
de aquel asombro infinito!
Y mientras no vengas tú
yo me quedaré en la orilla
de los vuelos, de los sueños,
de las estelas, inmóvil.
Porque sé que adonde estuve
ni alas, ni ruedas, ni velas
llevan.
Todas van extraviadas.

One reaches you only
through you. I wait for you.

Yes I know where I am,
my city, the street, the name
they all call me.
But I don't know where I was
with you.
You took me there.

How
was I to find out the road
when I was looking at nothing
but you,
when the road was your walk,
and the end
was when you stopped?
What more could I have than
what you offered gazing at me?

But now
what exile, what absence
it is to be where one is!
I wait. Trains go by,
chances, looks.
They would take me where
I've never been. But I
don't want new skies.
I want to be where I was.
With you, to be back.
What an immense newness
to go back again,
to repeat the never the same
infinite wonder!
And while you don't come
I'll stay on the shore
of flights, of dreams, in
stillness behind ship foam.
For I know that where I was
no wings, no wheels, no sails
take me.
All wander off.

Porque sé que adonde estuve
sólo
se va contigo, por ti.

· 60 ·   Tú no las puedes ver;
yo, sí.
Claras, redondas, tibias.
Despacio
se van a su destino;
despacio, por marcharse
más tarde de tu carne.
Se van a nada; son
eso no más, su curso.
Y una huella, a lo largo,
que se borra en seguida.
¿Astros?

Tú
no las puedes besar.
Las beso yo por ti.
Saben; tienen sabor
a los zumos del mundo.
¡Qué gusto negro y denso
a tierra, a sol, a mar!
Se quedan un momento
en el beso, indecisas
entre tu carne fría
y mis labios; por fin
las arranco. Y no sé
si es que eran para mí.
Porque yo no sé nada.
¿Son estrellas, son signos,
son condenas o auroras?
Ni en mirar ni en besar
aprendí lo que eran.
Lo que quieren se queda
allá atrás, todo incógnito.
Y su nombre también.

For I know that where I was
one only
goes to you through you.

You can't see them.
I can.
Bright, round, lukewarm.
Slowly
they go off to their destiny;
slowly to delay
leaving your flesh.
They go nowhere; they are
just that, their flow.
And a long trail
immediately rubbed out.
Stars?

You
can't kiss them.
I kiss them for you.
They taste. They've got the taste
of the world's juices.
What a black thick taste
of earth, of sun, of sea!
They stick a second
in a kiss—indecisive
between your chilly flesh
and my lips; finally
I rip them out. And I don't know
if they were for me.
For I know nothing.
Are they stars, signals,
penalties or daybreaks?
Not looking or kissing
did I learn what they were.
What they want stays
there behind, a mystery.
And their name too.

(Si las llamara lágrimas
nadie me entendería.)

· 61 ·   ¡Si tú supieras que ese
gran sollozo que estrechas
en tus brazos, que esa
lágrima que tú secas
besándola,
vienen de ti, son tú,
dolor de ti hecho lágrimas
mías, sollozos míos!

Entonces
ya no preguntarías
al pasado, a los cielos,
a la frente, a las cartas,
qué tengo, por qué sufro.
Y toda silenciosa,
con ese gran silencio
de la luz y el saber,
me besarías más,
y desoladamente.
Con la desolación
del que no tiene al lado
otro ser, un dolor
ajeno; del que está
sólo ya con su pena.
Queriendo consolar
en un otro quimérico,
el gran dolor que es suyo.

· 62 ·   Cuando tú me elegiste
—el amor eligió—
salí del gran anónimo
de todos, de la nada.
Hasta entonces
nunca era yo más alto
que las sierras del mundo.

(If I called them tears
no one would hear me.)

· 61 · If you knew that this
sob confined to
your arms, that
tear you dry
kissing it,
come from you, are you,
pain from you become tears,
mine, my sobs!

Then
you would not ask
the past, skies,
forehead, letters,
what's wrong, why I suffer.
And total quiet,
with that quietness
of light and knowledge,
you would kiss me more,
desolately.
With a desolation
that beside it has not
another being, an alien
pain; that is
now alone with its pain.
Wanting to console
in a chimerical other
the great sorrow that is his.

· 62 · When you chose me—
love chose—
I came out of the great anonymity
from everyone, from nothing.
Till then
I was never taller than
the sierras of the world.

[113]

Nunca bajé más hondo
de las profundidades
máximas señaladas
en las cartas marinas.
Y mi alegría estaba
triste, como lo están
esos relojes chicos,
sin brazo en que ceñirse
y sin cuerda, parados.
Pero al decirme: «tú»
—a mí, sí, a mí, entre todos—,
más alto ya que estrellas
o corales estuve.
Y mi gozo
se echó a rodar, prendido
a tu ser, en tu pulso.
Posesión tú me dabas
de mí, al dárteme tú.
Viví, vivo. ¿Hasta cuándo?
Sé que te volverás
atrás. Cuando te vayas
retornaré a ese sordo
mundo, sin diferencias,
del gramo, de la gota,
en el agua, en el peso.
Uno más seré yo
al tenerte de menos.
Y perderé mi nombre,
mi edad, mis señas, todo
perdido en mí, de mí.
Vuelto al osario inmenso
de los que no se han muerto
y ya no tienen nada
que morirse en la vida.

· 63 ·   No quiero que te vayas,
dolor, última forma
de amar. Me estoy sintiendo
vivir cuando me dueles
no en ti, ni aquí, más lejos:
en la tierra, en el año

I never sank deeper
than the maximum
depths marked out
on maritime charts.
And my gladness was
sad, as small watches are
without a wrist to fasten to,
without a winding crown, stopped.
But when you said: *you*,
to me, yes, to me singled out,
I was higher than stars,
deeper than coral.
And my joy
began to spin, caught
in your being, in your pulse.
You gave me possession of myself
when you gave your self to me.
I lived. I live. How long?
I know you will back out.
When you go
I will go back to a deaf
world that does not distinguish
gram or drop
in weight or water.
I'll be one more—like the rest—
when you are lost.
I'll lose my name,
my age, my gestures, all
lost in me, from me.
Gone back to the immense bone heap
of those who have not died
and now have nothing
to die for in life.

· 63 ·   I don't want you to go,
pain, last form
of loving. I feel myself
live when you hurt me
not in you, not here, but far off:
in land, in the year

[115]

de donde vienes tú,
en el amor con ella
y todo lo que fue.
En esa realidad
hundida que se niega
a sí misma y se empeña
en que nunca ha existido,
que sólo fue un pretexto
mío para vivir.
Si tú no me quedaras,
dolor, irrefutable,
yo me lo creería;
pero me quedas tú.
Tu verdad me asegura
que nada fue mentira.
Y mientras yo te sienta,
tú me serás, dolor,
la prueba de otra vida
en que no me dolías.
La gran prueba, a lo lejos,
de que existió, que existe,
de que me quiso, sí,
de que aún la estoy queriendo.

· 64 · ¡Qué de pesos inmensos,
órbitas celestiales,
se apoyan
—maravilla, milagro—,
en aires, en ausencias,
en papeles, en nada!
Roca descansa en roca,
cuerpos yacen en cunas,
en tumbas; ni las islas
nos engañan, ficciones
de falsos paraísos,
flotantes sobre el agua.
Pero a ti, a ti, memoria
de un ayer que fue carne
tierna, materia viva,
y que ahora ya no es nada
más que peso infinito,

where you come from,
in her love
and all that was.
In that drowned
reality that denies
itself and claims
it never was,
that it was only my
pretext for living.
If you did not stick with me,
irrefutable sorrow,
I might agree.
But you stick with me.
Your truth assures me
that nothing was a lie.
Pain, while I feel you,
you will be
proof of another life
when you did not ache.
The great proof, far away,
that she was, that she is,
that she loved me, yes,
that I go on loving her.

· 64 ·   What gigantic weight,
celestial bodies—
wonder, miracle—
are supported by
winds, absences,
paper, nothing!
Rock rests on rock,
bodies lie in cradles,
in tombs; islands don't
fool us, fictions
of false paradise
floating on the water.
But you, you, memory
of a past that was gentle
flesh, live matter
and now is nothing
but infinite weight,

[117]

gravitación, ahogo,
dime, ¿quién te sostiene
si no es la esperanzada
soledad de la noche?
A ti, afán de retorno,
anhelo de que vuelvan
invariablemente,
exactas a sí mismas,
las acciones más nuevas
que se llaman futuro,
¿quién te va a sostener?
Signos y simulacros
trazados en papeles
blancos, verdes, azules,
querrían ser tu apoyo
eterno, ser tu suelo,
tu prometida tierra.
Pero, luego, más tarde,
se rompen —unas manos—,
se deshacen, en tiempo,
polvo, dejando sólo
vagos rastros fugaces,
recuerdos, en las almas.
¡Sí, las almas, finales!
¡Las últimas, las siempre
elegidas, tan débiles,
para sostén eterno
de los pesos más grandes!
Las almas, como alas
sosteniéndose solas
a fuerza de aleteo
desesperado, a fuerza
de no pararse nunca,
de volar, portadoras
por el aire, en el aire,
de aquello que se salva.

· 65 ·   No en palacios de mármol,
no en meses, no, ni en cifras,
nunca pisando el suelo:
en leves mundos frágiles

gravity, oppression,
tell me, who holds you up
if it is not the hoped for
loneliness of the night?
And you, hunger
for return,
invariably,
precisely the same,
of fresh new actions
we call future,
who can hold you up?
Signs and semblances
traced on whites, greens, blues,
scraps of paper
would like to be your eternal
support, to be your floor,
your promised earth.
But then, later,
they break—some hands,
they come apart, in time,
dust, leaving only
vague illusive traces,
memories in the soul.
Yes, souls, the last ones!
The ultimate, always
select, weak,
eternal fulcrum
of the heaviest weights.
Souls like wings
upheld alone
by desperate fluttering,
by never stopping,
by flying, carriers
through the air, in the air,
of what can be saved.

· 65 ·   Not in marble palaces,
        not in months, no, nor in ciphers
        never touching the floor:
        we have lived together

[119]

hemos vivido juntos.
El tiempo se contaba
apenas por minutos:
un minuto era un siglo,
una vida, un amor.
Nos cobijaban techos,
menos que techos, nubes;
menos que nubes, cielos;
aun menos, aire, nada.
Atravesando mares
hechos de veinte lágrimas,
diez tuyas y diez mías,
llegábamos a cuentas
doradas de collar,
islas limpias, desiertas,
sin flores y sin carne;
albergue, tan menudo,
en vidrio, de un amor
que se bastaba él solo
para el querer más grande
y no pedía auxilio
a los barcos ni al tiempo.
Galerías enormes
abriendo
en los granos de arena,
descubrimos las minas
de llamas o de azares.
Y todo
colgando de aquel hilo
que sostenía, ¿quién?
Por eso nuestra vida
no parece vivida:
desliz, resbaladora,
ni estelas ni pisadas
dejó detrás. Si quieres
recordarla, no mires
donde se buscan siempre
las huellas y el recuerdo.
No te mires al alma,
a la sombra, a los labios.

in fragile delicate worlds.
Time was scarcely
counted in minutes;
a minute was a century,
a life, a love.
Roofs sheltered us,
they were less roofs than clouds,
less clouds than skies,
they were air, nothing.
Crossing oceans
made of twenty tears,
ten yours and ten mine,
we came to gold
necklace beads,
clean islands, deserted,
without flowers or beasts;
a tiny glass
harbor of love
was enough
for the greatest love,
and it asked
no help from ships or time.
Enormous galleries
opening up
in grains of sand,
where we discovered mines
of fire and surprise.
And all
hanging from a thread
that was holding up—who?
That's why our life
does not seem lived:
it slipped away,
no wake or steps
behind. If you want
to recall it, don't gaze
where one always looks
for traces and memory.
Don't look at the soul,
at darkness, at lips.

Mírate bien la palma
de la mano, vacía.

Lo encontraremos, sí.
Nuestro beso. ¿Será
en un lecho de nubes,
de vidrios o de ascuas?
¿Será
este minuto próximo,
o mañana, o el siglo
por venir, o en el borde
mismo ya del jamás?
¿Vivos, muertos? ¿Lo sabes?
¿Con tu carne y la mía,
con mi nombre y el tuyo?
¿O ha de ser ya con otros
labios, con otros nombres
y siglos después, esto
que está queriendo ser
hoy, aquí, desde ahora?
Eso no lo sabemos.
Sabemos que será.
Que en algo, sí, y en alguien
se tiene que cumplir
este amor que inventamos
sin tierra ni sin fecha
donde posarse ahora:
el gran amor en vilo.
Y que quizá, detrás
de telones de años,
un beso bajo cielos
que jamás hemos visto,
será, sin que lo sepan
esos que creen dárselo,
trascendido a su gloria,
el cumplirse, por fin,
de ese beso impaciente
que te veo esperando,
palpitante en los labios.
Hoy

Look carefully into the palm
of your hand, empty.

We will find it, yes.
Our kiss. Maybe
in a bed of clouds,
of glass or burning coals.
Maybe
in the next minute
or tomorrow or in the coming
century or on the very edge
of what is never.
Live, dead? Do you know?
With your flesh and mine,
my name and yours?
Or must it now be with
other lips, other names
and centuries after
what longs to be
today, here, from now on?
We don't know that.
We know it will be.
In something, yes, in someone
will come
a love we invented
without land or date
where it can be now.
A huge love in the air.
And maybe from behind
the curtain of years,
will come
a kiss under never seen skies,
unknown to those
who think they are kissing,
rising into luminosity,
to achieve at last
that impatient kiss
I see you waiting for,
throbbing on your lips.
Today

nuestro beso, su lecho,
están sólo en la fe.

· 67 ·   ¿Quién, quién me puebla el mundo
esta noche de agosto?
No, ni carnes, ni alma.
Faroles, contra luna.
¿Abrazarme? ¿Con quién?
¿Seguir? ¿A quién? Veloces
coincidencias de astro
y gas lo suplen todo.
Sombras y yo. Y el aire
meciendo blandamente
el cabello a las sombras
con un rumor de alma.
Me acercaré a su lecho
—aire quieto, agua quieta—
a intentar que me quieran
a fuerza de silencio
y de beso. Engañado
hasta que venga el día
y el gran lecho vacío
donde durmieron ellas,
sin huellas de la carne,
y el gran aire vacío,
limpio,
sin señal de las almas,
otra vez me confirmen
la soledad, diciendo
que todo eran encuentros
fugaces, aquí abajo
de las luces distantes,
azares sin respuesta.
No, ni carnes, ni almas.

· 68 ·   ¡Qué cuerpos leves, sutiles,
hay, sin color,
tan vagos como las sombras,
que no se pueden besar
si no es poniendo los labios

our kiss, its bed,
lies only in faith.

· 67 ·   Who? Who can people the world
for me on this August night?
No. Neither body nor soul.
Street lamps against the moon.
Hug me? Who?
Pursue her? Whom? Rapid
coincidences of star
and gas take the place.
Shadows and me. And air
blandly swaying
the shadow's hair
with a sound of soul.
I will go to her bed—
quiet air, quiet water—
to try to make them want me
through silence
and kiss. Tricked
until the day comes
and the big empty bed
where they were sleeping
with no sign of flesh
in the great air empty,
clean,
with no sign from the souls,
they will again confirm
my solitude, saying
that it was all furtive
meetings, here under
far lights,
an unresponding gamble.
No. No flesh nor souls.

· 68 ·   What subtle light bodies
there are,
colorless, inconcrete like shadows,
that can't be kissed
except by putting your lips

[125]

en el aire, contra algo
que pasa y que se parece!

¡Y qué sombras tan morenas
hay, tan duras
que su oscuro mármol frío
jamás se nos rendirá
de pasión entre los brazos!

¡Y qué trajín, ir, venir,
con el amor en volandas,
de los cuerpos a las sombras,
de lo imposible a los labios,
sin parar, sin saber nunca
si es alma de carne o sombra
de cuerpo lo que besamos,
si es algo! ¡Temblando
de dar cariño a la nada!

· 69 ·   ¿Y si no fueran las sombras
sombras? ¿Si las sombras fueran
—yo las estrecho, las beso,
me palpitan encendidas
entre los brazos—
cuerpos finos y delgados,
todos miedosos de carne?

¡Y si hubiese
otra luz más en el mundo
para sacarles a ellas,
cuerpos ya de sombra, otras
sombras más últimas, sueltas
de color, de forma, libres
de sospecha de materia;
y que no se viesen ya
y que hubiera que buscarlas
a ciegas, por entre cielos,
desdeñando ya las otras,
sin escuchar ya las voces
de esos cuerpos disfrazados
de sombras, sobre la tierra?

in the air, against something
passing by and that resembles them.

And what brown shadows,
so hard
that their cold dark marble
will never fall
passionately in our arms!

And what going and coming,
with love flying about,
from bodies to shadows,
from impossibility to lips,
ceaselessly, never knowing
if it is soul, flesh, or shadow
of a body that we kiss,
if anything at all! Terrified
of caressing nothing!

· 69 ·   If shadows were not
shadows? If shadows were—
I grab them, kiss them—
they burn me shaking
in their arms—
slim fine bodies,
all frightened of flesh?

And if there were
other light in the world
to draw out of them
bodies of shadows, other
more complete shadows, empty
of color, form, free
of the suspicion of matter;
and unseen,
that one could look for
blind through the heavens
now despising others,
and not hear voices
from those masked bodies
of shadows on the earth?

[127]

¿Las oyes cómo piden realidades,
ellas, desmelenadas, fieras,
ellas, las sombras que los dos forjamos
en este inmenso lecho de distancias?
Cansadas ya de infinitud, de tiempo
sin medida, de anónimo, heridas
por una gran nostalgia de materia,
piden límites, días, nombres.
No pueden
vivir así ya más: están al borde
del morir de las sombras, que es la nada.
Acude, ven, conmigo.
Tiende tus manos, tiéndeles tu cuerpo.
Los dos les buscaremos
un color, una fecha, un pecho, un sol.
Que descansen en ti, sé tú su carne.
Se calmará su enorme ansia errante,
mientras las estrechamos
ávidamente entre los cuerpos nuestros
donde encuentren su pasto y su reposo.
Se dormirán al fin en nuestro sueño
abrazado, abrazadas. Y así luego,
al separarnos, al nutrirnos sólo
de sombras, entre lejos,
ellas
tendrán recuerdos ya, tendrán pasado
de carne y hueso,
el tiempo que vivieron en nosotros.
Y su afanoso sueño
de sombras, otra vez, será el retorno
a esta corporeidad mortal y rosa
donde el amor inventa su infinito.

Do you hear how they beg for realities,
those disheveled terrible beasts,
they, the shadows that we both forge
in this great bed of distances?
Tired now of infinity, of loose
time, of anonymity, and wounds
from an intense nostalgia for matter,
they ask for limits, days, names.
They can't
live this way any longer: they are at the edge
of the death of shadows, that is nothingness.
Come near, come with me.
Stretch out your hands, offer your body.
We two will look for a color
for them, a date, a chest, a sun.
Let them relax in you, you be their flesh.
Their enormous roaming hunger will calm
while we clutch them
greedily between our bodies
where they will find pasture and repose.
They will sleep at last in our dream,
in our embrace. And so, then,
when we go apart, when we nourish only
on shadows, caught in distances,
they will have memories now, a past
of flesh and bone:
the time when they lived in us.
And their starving dream
of shadows will be the return again
to a mortal and pink body
where love invents its infinity.

Letter
Poems
to
Katherine

A shattering. A woman. A Katherine,
is stuck in a wooden drawer among unknown
beings, before a sad and concealed night.

One must leave her there. Fatally. And
the other woman, the other Katherine,
remains invisible, present, beside me,

comes with me, happily hanging on my arm,
looking at me with her noble glance, pure
and deep as always. In the rail station,

in the goodbye, there is no simple separation
of one being from another. No. Each of us left
not only the other beloved creature

but also that part of us that she loves
and that departs with her. Isn't it true? Last night
you didn't cut off from me, nor I from you.

Rather, I split from myself, I feel it now,
and you the same. Today, last night, today I sense
that I am walking among ghosts and shadows,

with someone alongside me I cannot hug,
but who lives surrounding me, who escapes
each time I try to grab her. An anguished

yet sweet sensation, a shattered caress.
And horror in those last minutes, knocked down
by stupidity and chaos. I hated

that ignoble slime, I'd lash them, hurl all
of them out to make a place, a great place,
a whole train for you!   When you left, my senses

were at ease. Do you know why? In my pocket
next to my chest I felt the lump of your letter.
They lie who say paper has no weight! Last night

the paper of your letter pulled me down
like the handsomest and gravest reality.
I felt it in my pocket like tangible proof

of you being there and that you had existed.
Because, do you know? I began to doubt.
Doubt all, your reality, mine, of the world,

of the last days . . . only the bulk of your letter
was a pledge, proof. I lived on that rectangle
of paper. Safest spot in the world. Before

I could open it, locked and in my pocket,
your letter was the bridge to life, and yes,
gave life to the tormenting question: Am I?

Is it? Are we? Yes, yes, yes. Everything,
yes, listen, everything yes. Then in my room
I read it. I have read it. I shall read it.

What delights! First the delight of taking in
your handwriting, your letters, of stumbling
on a word and finally deciphering it.

Your handwriting, another mode of you,
another way of living you! Your first letter,
in English. Jubilance, jubilance, pleasure.

Festival sensation, inaugural of promise,
of fiesta! No matter that your letter
is stained with a shadow of melancholy

tender and soft. It had to be like that.
But beyond that melancholy, there is
something that gives me unbounded joy:

"You have taken away the cynicism
that was growing upon me." Can it be?
Do I have the luck of being elected

in a difficult moment of your life
to save you from something? What a boost
for my role at your side for my company!

Now it is not egoism that I follow
distantly in your life. It is for your good.
I can be spiritually useful. I am preparing

for this splendid task: to help you live,
to pull you out of negative forces,
from shadowy powers threatening you.

And that is for you, not for me. Get it?
Oh, if you might do me this favor, to let
me serve you! What a right thing, that you,

who do not grasp such enthusiasm for life,
may through me have it returned to you,
an enthusiasm which is yours. No, no,

you were not born for cynical skepticism
nor self-deceptive frivolity. Never
surrender to that. I can't imagine you

parading your spleen on the terraces
of grand hotels with some insignificant
escort. Never. Believe in yourself. In

your supreme distinction, in the nobility
of your soul. And live for it. Whether far off
or nearby, it will help you. Until you have no

further need. And look, hear me, don't fear
that I might be taking something away
from someone by loving you, no. You say so

so delicately in your letter! No,
I am not and will not be worse for anyone
because of you, no. What you ask me, what

I give you in no way affects what I owe
to others. You in me will never be
anything bad, nothing I might rob from

another, no. Don't fear. Each day I will be
better. You have lighted in me new riches
and so what I give, you take from no one.

Do you understand? Don't suffer over that.
You are pure, loyal, a brightness. From you
comes only the high light of paradise.

Madrid Tuesday, 1 August 1932 (1)

YESTERDAY THE CLASS AGAIN A FORM OF FLIGHT

Yesterday the class again a form of flight,
and more painful when she was there,
when it was the place designated by gods, yes, yes,
by gods! For your appearance on earth.
Magic instant, unforgettable when I saw surge,
out of nothing, eyes, lips, a body,
a human and behind her I felt intact light quiver,
pure, new, with life! I assure you that Mythology
which I adore has nothing of this perfection.

No birth of Venus, no Greek relief sculpture,
no Botticelli, has that passion, that oceanic feeling
as seeing you being born from I don't know where,
from oblivion, from the nonexistent, from sky,
or rather from yourself. Yes, you were born
from yourself. I first saw your bodily appearance,
a sign, a sign of promise. Little by little,
I saw your own flesh; from your own figure
came a new being, was born a revelatory creature.

Prodigy, miracle, astonishment!
And rarest of all she verified it, it happened,
and no one realized but me—not even you—
in a place which has nothing of miracle.

No one saw anything, no one said a thing.
But that night on leaving the class,
the world held a new illusion, a new yearning.
I assure you I thought you would never know.
I thought you would pass by me and I could not
come near your holy stature, far and superior
like goddesses and intense desires.

Would you know one day? I wondered.
You must know how I saved you in me
from others, from the rest. Now I wonder,
Do you know it, know it, know it?

Pedro
Madrid Tuesday, 1 August 1932 (2)

I REREAD YOUR LETTERS

I reread your letters. I looked for you
through them, the letter, the words.
Your letters are like an enchanted wood.
In everything one notes you have passed by;
the ground, the trees, the light keep
your echo, the perfume of your step.

I go along, lost, saying, "She is near,
now I'll find her, she just passed by,
I see her footprints." The whole wood
is filled with your presence. But you
are missing. I don't find you. I go ahead,
ahead, cross through the forest,
and you only live in footprints, echoes,
shadows, but you escape from me
among the single letters. I go back,
read and reread the letter, which is
to race through the forest to see if,
now, on turning a page, on returning
to a phrase, I find you, divine,
in body and soul, asleep, as in me,
mythological fable. How stupid!

Really? What hurt is that I feel that you
are to travel through Spain, maybe
near where I may be! Don't you know
how I would run, how I would come!
And why not do it?, I wonder.
Worry about career, a brakeless car,
a mad flight? What nonsense, pardon!

Tell me where you are traveling to,
give me dates, hotel names, all
that's possible so at least I can speak
to you on the phone. If you pass by
Alicante, the city, tell me so, don't
forget to. Tear up, tear up this letter,
it is the most absurd, the craziest of all,
tear it up, but keep me, because
I'm afraid, afraid. From what do you
not keep me? You know from what.
I already told you the other day.

Pedro

[In the margins]

What joy in writing to you today,
saving this moment of a stupid day,
I needed to write you, to rob time of
so-called business, and offer you time
as a salvation of myself. Tear it up,
tear this up. Pardon the letter. It's worse
than ever. Can you understand that?

Madrid 9 of August 1932 (5)

WHAT TERRIBLE EAGERNESS TO SEE YOU!

What terrible eagerness to *see you!*
Clearly I don't call seeing you looking
at you near me, putting my physical eyes
on you. No. I call *seeing you* as you appear

like this, in your absence, in my soul,
like and how you are, like and how I saw
you in reality. I can't. And it is torture.

I know by memory, by heart memory,
all I might resort to for describing you.
Each feature, each physical line I know
in its essential beauty. Color of your eyes,
line of your forehead, your mouth,
whimsy of your walk, sound of your voice.

Everything, everything I know. I do not lack
any data. Yet what pain in not being able
to manage to touch your very being,
with its components! I assure you it is
a true labor of soul. I seek your *I*,
your *totality*, your being, by way of
the appearances that compose it
and that I possess. And I never find it.

It is a true mania. I begin the labor
for the eyes, more work for the folds
of the nose—which you claim is ugly!
More for your way of walking. I seek
trails, roads, entries, and all in vain.
I never achieve your full revelation.

If you could see how happy I am at time
with just this! (Maybe to console myself.)
I say happy because in this way I know
I am not inventing an imaginary Katherine
in my fantasy, independently of you.
No. My Katherine has need of your reality.
Need of your own vision, of your
unsubstitutable being. It is no dream,
no illusion. It is not the product
of my passionate imagination.
It is a live woman who walks, who breathes,
who feels. And without her her whole image
is imperfect. You are your own image.

Understand? You are you. You and your image
all at once. Always when I look at you,
Katherine, I've seen you in you, and beyond you,
in your second and ultimate you. Is this
a madness? No, no. My supreme pleasure
is having discovered that *double* of you.

That's what I call your image. Now that image
of yours only is revealed in your presence.
That's why you give so much. Do you see?
When I look at you I am enriched not only
with what I see, but with what I see beyond.

But without you, neither reality nor image.
Only signs. Signs of you, signals of your
existence, *probabilities*. You when far
are only *probable*. Do you understand
my pain? Understand my furious search
through memories of your forms to encounter
the *certain*. Do you see how you live in me?

With all my spiritual forces unchained,
you throw them into commotion, into
the leftovers of being. You are, Katherine,
a motive of my life, in the pure sense
of the term. I know that if I lacked a *motive*
the wings that have opened in me would close,
the many canticles I begin to hear
would be hushed, and the many dawns trembling
on the horizon would be extinguished.
So I am afraid, afraid, I tell you, because
it is true, and I am living one day less
now that I live more, which is thanks to you.

Pedro
El Altet Saturday 13? of August 1932 (6)

IN THE COUNTRYSIDE

In the countryside. On passing
through Alicante I pick up a letter.

Now I look for the one
in Madrid. I am sad, yes, sad.
From Madrid to Palma
lies a great terrain.

But from here, this shore,
it seems that behind the blue
of the horizon
is the precinct of land
where you live. Does
the sea join or sever?

With what a rare sensation
I read your letter! Yes,
Katherine, a beginning
I told you. So I want it
to be. Not an end. A start
especially for you.

Incipit vita nuova. A new life
of soul for you, and I on the sideline
as a point of departure from a life.
Will you always remember me as
a point of departure, Katherine?
I don't know if this new life
takes you away from me,
but always I'll be happy
you left me. It doesn't matter
that I am frozen still.

You must wander, Katherine,
and at some time glance
at the place you quit: me.
That is enough
for me. It is my recompense.

To see you live. What joy
to see you live, live a life
lofty and complete,
conscious of your worth
and beauty of soul!
Haven't you often thought

of those trees on river banks
that bend over the current
and, though nailed to the banks
permanently, they face
the river and waters
with their image for it
to be carried away into waves?

I think the water carts off
the soul of the tree,
the yearning for change,
its leaves, flower, flowing,
flowing down river,
and only leaves its material
form on earth.
I am really crazy!

Ask yourself, tell me
what I have thought up.
I do not want to
figure it out. I know.
Why do you doubt
what I have thought?
Don't you feel it in you?
I know it every second.

I can't let go of anything
of yours. Look, an example
is the letters. It would be
more prudent (forgive the word)
if I had not left them
in Madrid and those I get
to tear up. But I cannot,
no. I need to conserve
this form of your word,
of your life. To join
me to it as the only material
proof of truth. It would seem
to me the greatest cowardice

to tear them up. But beyond
cowardice I need them,
them, in real form,

as in you I need a multitude
of things in your real form.
Goodbye, Katherine.
I am upset, unquiet. Rest,
but I can't rest. I swim, like you,
I swim a lot, I push myself

till I'm exhausted. Yes, I repeat,
you live in me as a new force,
as a world of impulses,
desires, happiness, and new pain.
All, all. Suffering and joy,
spirit of pressure, spirit of renunciation,

everything. All human, but
sheltering in a being, in a creature,
flesh made soul. That I feel,
thank you, thank you for new life,
the start, yes the start
of I don't know what,

but something great in me,
an expansion of living,
enjoying, suffering all things.
I sign happier
because you
like my name.

Pedro
El Altet Saturday 14 August 1932 (7)

THANKS, THANKS FOR YOUR LETTERS

Thanks, thanks for your letters. I thank you,
all of them. From the instant you sit at the table
to write, from the movement that your hand makes

to pick up the pen, from what is finest
and most delicate that your soul infuses
in them. For me, all that, Katherine! Is it
possible? Outside around you must be sky,
sun or stars, beauty and silence; or lively
people, fun, society; or books and notes
waiting to be sent off. And you, Katherine,
choose me. You leave that to give me on paper
what you can't give me in presence. Living
is a constant choice. The world offers us
a vast repertory of beings and things;
one who truly lives must always select.

Do you understand how miraculous it is
that being among lovely things, one, two,
you pick up your pen and elect me? So
I thank you. So your letters are not for me
paper, not words, not thoughts. Much more.
Miracles that fall on me, and before them
I find myself startled, overwhelmed to be
me, among others, are designated for
your grace. You told me yesterday, "You are
my greatest reality." How I have lived
that phrase! How one lives in the sea, swimming
through it, letting me be saturated through it.

Do you know why those words have moved
me so? They are my certificate of existence.
I am a reality! I'm not a name, an employee,
a citizen, a shadow, a reflection, no. I am
reality. You say it to me. And with that I am,
you increase me, so I am reality in you.
My greatest reality. I feel proud, happy,
wanting to jump, run, live a lot.

Do you know, Katherine, that I doubt deeply
in my reality? In my *true* reality! Yes, I'm sure
of my physical and social reality,
of my age, of my names, of my duties
and functions. But the other, the intimate
and profound reality? Am I what I am?
Have I not been caught on the road

between false realities, the most precious
of all and what is radically mine?

Do I still exist, and am I, like many
people, pure mechanism, automaton,
a habit, nothing? To believe in our own
difference it is essential that someone believe
in us. We believe in us, Katherine, through
someone who believes in us. My reality
now, today, I feel it, I believe it, I love it,
because you believe in it. No, I am not shadow,
I am not that in me. I am my own reality
since what I am is my reality, because
it is the *greatest reality!* See? Sometimes I fear
my letters seem too serious and grave to you,
that you don't see in me the joking.

And I wonder, "How will she like that?"
But, Katherine, I cannot speak to you
in another way. You are for me something
so enormously serious! When I'm with you
I joke, laugh, make light conversation.
Because I see you by me and don't fear.
Because you can, just looking at me, see
what is behind. But now, remote, I want
you to see me as I am inside for you,
you know how. Isn't that true, *dearest, dearest.*

Pedro

[In the margins]

Yesterday or today I couldn't go to the city.
We have no car. I am all day thinking
if I'll have a letter. Tomorrow I will go
downtown to look, with whatever pretext.

El Altet Sunday 14 of August 1932 (8)

I write you from Alicante, in a hurry.
I came to look for your letters. Already
it's been three days without them.
I begin to worry. What could have happened?
Hypothesis. Fears. . . . But today a blue
envelope, a blue letter. I see you,
I see you in a tiny photograph.
But how small, how imperfect! One of thousands
of Katherines that comprise Katherine. More, more,
I want more. Thanks. I send you verses. New
ones, and those you have read. I read your letter
quickly, in the Nautical Club, where I
write you. As soon as I return to the
country I'll read it word by word, caress
by caress. Tarragona, Barcelona!

Good. Give me dates. If you like I'll send you
a letter for someone in Barcelona.
Dates, hotel names! I want to talk to you
by phone. I'll call you in all the cities
of Spain where you may go. Your voice, at least
your voice. I will send you more verses. Thanks
for what you say to me, for accepting them,
for giving me them. Excuse this letter.
I'm happy with yours. I'm going to read it.

Pedro
Alicante Tuesday 16 of August 1932 (9)

[In the margins]

Sorry I write you every day. I can't
do less. Do I tire you? Does my persistence
fatigue you? I fear I may tire you with me.

Dearest, I like you . . . and more, more, you know.

I'm leaving tonight. I can't stay any longer
in Barcelona. I don't want to sleep
again in this room. It would be futile

to try to sleep in it. I want to sleep
rolling, letting myself shoot off in the
opposite direction that you are taking,

but impelled by the same force, to return.
That is my consolation. Every step,
to the North, South, is now a step to you.

Fatally distance and time are mortal
enemies. But now I feel the defensive
forces slowly rising in me, the interior

labor for saving us against distance
and time. They themselves. But turned around.
Understand? The opposite directions we

are taking coincide at a point where
they are not in opposition. Gone beyond
all that. The day, the place where we can see

each other again. Living to live. Your hand
you extend to me like the last knot in the world
is the same hand you will extend at the

greeting of arrival. I'll never forget
the tears you didn't shed but which saw you
veiled with modesty, standing, loving me

with your whole glance. You couldn't love me
with less. Now not with a look, love, nor without
a look, now. With your beyond look, higher,

more powerful, with which I look at you.
I see you, and I will see you. We have found
many ways of loving. Now other. They will

not be lacking to me nor lacking to you.
No more. I recall your phrase: "I'm very
practical." (My poor little one, practical,

you, who fall in love with me, which is
the least practical thing in the world that one
can do!) I have gone out to eat. A pure

simulacrum. Attempts. Beer, a cigarette,
my two vices. Room 410. And then collapse.
Yes, crying, crying. And you immediately

show up to calm me. I'm saved. "Write me
what you would like me to see in Paris."
So I have done. And I've put down a few

stupidities in case you like them so you
won't see me sad. Now to pack up, go to bed
so I can leave Barcelona and walk through

the places, exactly the same ones where
we walked the other day. Nothing else.
Ah, yes, to buy some eau de cologne I forgot

to do and keep it to give to you as soon
as we see each other. Shall we end like this
today? Yes, it will be better, better

than to tell your face I see, the eyes I see
when I stand before the mirror and don't
recognize myself. Understand? I, the other
I don't know, but of whom, yes, love.

Pedro
Barcelona 27 Aug 1932 (12)

[postdated]

This night the two of us in the train, hearing
inside and out the same thing, iron, love.

[In the margins]

Do you see how excited I am writing you?
I won't weep any more.

YESTERDAY I KISSED YOU ON THE LIPS

Yesterday I kissed you on the lips.
I kissed you on the lips. Delicate,
red. It was such a quick kiss
that it lasted longer than lightning,
than a miracle, longer.
                              Time
after giving you this
was nothing
to me. I had wanted it
for nothing before.
It began and ended in the flash.

Today I kiss a kiss;
I am alone with my lips.
I put them
not in your mouth, no not now
—where did it get away to?—
I put them
in the kiss I gave you
yesterday, in our joined mouths
of the kiss they kissed.

And this kiss lasts longer
than silence, than light.
For it is no longer flesh
or a mouth I kiss,
that slips away, escapes from me.
No.
I am kissing you further away.

August? 1932 (16) [earlier version of poem 36]

For the first time I write on an envelope:
Prospect Street. Your house! My letter must know
all. Know all that I don't know,
that I would like to know. What is Northampton
like? And your street? I must climb
the stairway of your house, go in through the door
you go in through, come into your bedroom.
And the letter that goes, that walks, that arrives
has no eyes, and blind it can't see
what I with open eyes, dying to see, can't see
either. Do I envy it or not?
Who will come closer to you, it or I?

Is it better to be the material
beside you, though it's deaf, blind, or a soul
that is remote, alive, awake,
loving you? Better me or my letter?
I don't know. The two incompletes,
the letter and me. But what desire, envy
to be able to be in your hand,
below your eyes, alive through the light
of your glance, like these letters.

All that luck this piece of paper has, passive,
that you pick up. It doesn't know it.
While I, Katherine! . . . now I remember
I recall a phrase I heard in a train
from an Andalusian youth who was bitching
the whole way, saying, how far off
it all is . . . Yes, it's true, how far off it is.
And between this huge distance,
this bridge of paper each day I hold up for you
over all, so over all a soul may cross
over with all its desires, its illusions, its loving.
I sent you a radiogram I suppose
you got on the *Columbus*, with these words: *Always,
wonder*. What childlike joy I felt
at your surprise in getting it! You know,
it was a wild venture. Spain! Though

it seems a lie, at the Telegraph Office in Alicante
no one had ever sent a cable
to a ship going to America. They rummaged
through God knows how many books
and charges, for ten minutes they stared at me
with mad astonishment. And I
who wanted to pass unnoticed, they made me
famous in the Telegraph Office.
But you must know I could not surrender
to silence. I had to talk to you
and somehow hurl my words over the sea . . .

Pedro
El Altet Saturday Sept 10 (22)

And were you lost, I would be,
Though my name
Rang loudest
On the heavenly fame.

And were you saved,
And I condemned to be
Where you were not,
That self were hell to me.

So we must keep apart,
You there, I here,
With just the door ajar
That oceans are,
And prayer,
And that pale sustenance,
Despair!

[by Emily Dickinson]

What if say I shall not wait?
What if I burst the fleshly gate
And I pass, escaped, to thee?
What if I file this mortal uff [sic],
See where it hurt me,—that's enough—,
And wade in liberty?

[by Emily Dickinson]

THINKING OF YOU, ALWAYS

Thinking of you, always, all day long.
Like never.
I accuse myself of blowing up unreasonably
the worth of your words.
Tormented still, but happy because the torment
comes from my great love.
Tomorrow I'll write you,
as it were, a confession letter loading
on you my state these days.
Beautiful Goethe phrase:
Who doesn't know despair doesn't live.
Because I despair, I hope.
Thanks, thanks, Katherine, from your

Pedro
Madrid Monday 31 October (24)

YESTERDAY

Yesterday, my Katherine, I ended up seized
by poor Pedro. Can you forgive me, soul?

How much you will have to forgive if you keep on
loving this man who persists on loving you.

But today I want to make corrections.
To erase the passion. To speak *coldly*.

(Doesn't it make you smile, me coldly?)
This is a vain aspiration of being like me

who is professionally an intellectual,
and temperamentally all passion,

believing only in instinct, in miracle.
. . . .

Pedro

And something else more delicate and hard.
Do you think a man like me, who loves you

as I do, who *adores* you, who wants for you
the most tender delicacy, can say this:

When you come to Europe, I beg you
to let me send the round trip ship ticket.

I've been thinking about it since September.
I might have told you then, but it's the same.

I know you know me, now you look at me
face to face. Do you see me? It would be

so fraternal, so familiar, so simply done!
You would show me there is nothing

between us that's not of us two. *Understand*
that I don't want you to drop coming to Europe

for material reasons. Never. I don't know
your circumstances, but I'd be desperate

to think that your wish to come be limited,
restricted by a material fact. *It's no work*

at all for me. Concede that to me, Katherine,
I beg you. You understand my total love.

Nothing gets away from it. Listen. You'll drink
in the same glass as me, eat the same fruit

I have started. No? Nothing alien between us.
Katherine, I trust you absolutely, know

you understand me, without doubt. True?
Do what I ask, and finally, accept or not,

but for God, for our love, understand
the cleanness with which *I speak to you.*

Madrid Thursday 3 November (26)

YESTERDAY AN ACUTE MOST VIVID SENSATION

Yesterday an acute most vivid sensation
of my new *state,* of the new being I am
since August. These days are the days of the dead

and I have the custom of going each year
to bring flowers to the tomb of my parents.
I always like to go alone. It is like a return

in memory to this world of my childhood
now sunk and the most remote in time.
And while it seems stupid I have the illusion

of examining my consciousness, not religious,
purely human; of a confrontation between me
and the past and future. That works fine

in the cemetery. It is a cemetery now closed,
somewhat melancholy, very 19th century
(even one destined to eternity has a seal

of the period!). I sit in the sun a while,
renounce haste and even haste renounces me.
I release my thoughts. Do you know what

I let out? A confidence, in silence, of all
I feel. Confidence to whom? I don't know.
To my parents buried there? I think not.

Rather to part of oneself also buried in time,
if not in earth. My I of yesterday. That I
for which earlier I went to the cemetery

and which felt done with, having gone through
part of my life, yet hangs on to a great eagerness
to keep living. But this year, Katherine! You

came to me, as in all places. There where
so many tender things fed you accompanied me,
total proof of the empowerment of my soul

through your image. There I felt the blessing
of loving, of happiness, of loving with all
my soul, or reliving right next to the exact

forces of the past, for what might come,
for what might come from you and from my love.
How good to confront oneself in this way,

from time to time, with the past and with death!
It is like taking your vital pressure just as
a doctor takes your arterial blood pressure.

Vital tension, that is, capacity, flexibility
in the canals of life, the arteries of life,
that lead to the forces to remain alive!

How often in these last years I have felt,
my soul, low in pressure, without faith
in my vital arterial system! Inclined

to give up, to cede, to that terrible thing
of just *going on being,* rather that *to be.*
But now, yesterday, my vital pressures—

the past, the sun, the wind, solitude—
took it, gripping me like the doctor my pulse,
and I felt firm, more willful than ever.

I want to live and not just go on living!
I am, I am, my Katherine, who confirms
I am. And while she loves me I will be

a new man who yesterday thanked life,
who desired it entirely, there in that place
where it ends. Thanks to you.

[no signature]

[In the margins]

Six days without a letter! I can't wait any longer.
Am beginning to shiver, to think only of what
could have gone wrong. Sick? Absent-minded?
Oh, forgive. How you may have got mine yesterday?
Does it bother you? Do understand, my God.

Madrid 14 November Friday (27)

HOW YOUR ABSENCE WEIGHS ME DOWN!

How your absence weighs me down!
You! with your body, you never were a weight,
you gave the world wings!
But now! I feel something on me, drowning me,
suffocating me,
and it is you I miss, whom I don't have.
Your flesh, your body were light,
were air, not matter,
so beautiful in its adored kissed matter.
Not having her, not kissing her,
is my weight and what crushes me.

Pedro
Sunday 6 November, 2 in the afternoon (29)

I GO DOWNTOWN

I go downtown to see if there are letters!
Thanks, thanks! Now happiness, life,
all comes back.

[155]

How I would hold you in my arms, today,
crazy, crazy, crazy to thank you for the cable,
for everything! How stupid I am!
Aren't I? If I could hold you in my arms
there'd be no cable, no letters!
I'm happy like a child.
Today I too will leave here like you the other day,
like my breeze. Like wind with no road,
loose happiness,
free because of blessed Katherine center of my life,
my life, you, your

Pedro
[Tomorrow I'll write you more reasonably.]

Sunday 6 November, later same day (29)

IN THE TRAIN. FROM PALENCIA TO MADRID

How gray, how brown, how austere this Castilla
I'm crossing while I write you. On the last trip
a month ago in my letter I sent the golds of poplars
bidding goodbye to leaves. Today only branches, skeletons,

and all Castilla appears peopled by erect skeletons.
What can I send you today? I must see golds inside.
If I send what encircles me it will be gray sky,
brown earth, denuded trunks, winter, Castilla.

That hurts. Since all we Castilians have gold in us
and slope into the grave huge sadness of our land.
Resignation, solitude, melancholy and dignified
renunciation. But I don't yield, don't renounce,

I don't want to be alone, no. In me the gold leaves
of the poplars are still alive. And two kinds. Those
I saw a month ago, the last gold ones, others from
last summer when I found you. And greening ones

that in four months will pop out to flourish through
the summer. The trees don't feel any of these.

They are naked foliage. But I have two in me:
that were and will come. I arm myself against landscape,

Castilla, against season, winter, and center in me
every hope. How good to feel inside an entity
that rejects the wounded and desolate imposition
of the external! To feel a reason for life, a need

to blossom, beating within. My heart, you know it,
is you. You are what beats in me with the fire
of life. What guards me from my defeat before
dry and nude Castilla. You go at my side, become

summers, suns, glows, lights, protecting me
so the cold won't enter me, the desolation of land
in the soul. You are the anti-earth. The raiser,
who raises me suspended as on wings

beyond the emaciated ground, oil of landscape,
and you make me sense I do not belong
to this cold, past, gray, but to that faith,
future, ecstasy. Thank you, Katherine.

I hope your love never tires of saving me
against the cold, more winters, desolations.
May the land not have dominion over me.
Let me never, soul, be without your wings.

Pedro
Wednesday 14 December (43)

END OF THE DAY!

End of the day! At last, end of the day!
The maddening tasks, endless junk
    and *tangent world*.

Light out in my room. Only the lamp
that lights me so I can write to you.
    No more light

than what I need for you and me.
The rest in shadow. I delight in this.
   I look around

and my gaze penetrates nothing.
A momentary abolition of what
   is not the desk,

your letters, spread out around me,
this paper. I have the intimately delicious
   sensation of

burning our world, of extinguishing
the remaining earth. There are borders.
   borders of light,

for our realm of light. Far from the vast
conjunction of world and space, some
   square centimeters,

and island. Our island, this light,
of this night. Beyond, deaf, enormous,
   surrounding us,

the rest. But here, Katherine,
I tell you are only two beings
   like a kiss.

Almost the feeling of kiss. Lamp, light,
and writing you, the same: island of two.
   What a find!

I once wrote, "We have lived together
in fragile delicate worlds." Another one
   this night. "How

to thank you, soul, for this beauty
of each instant I feel living beside you,
   in which I don't live

alone but in the deep pleasure
of a love accompanying my
    loneliness!"

I'm going to write you. Blessed words!
I'll scrawl them again. I am going
    to write you.

I relish them. I don't yet know what
I'll scribble, who cares? But know as day
    ends there is

no weariness without escape. Final
weariness, but a new force. An impulse
    moves my hand

to put on the light, to grab the paper,
to pick up the pen. And all these tiny
    insignificant acts

are *sacred*, yes! Because in them
is revelation, a divinity,
    your love.

Pedro
Madrid 20 December Tuesday (47)

MY LETTERS SEEM TO ME POETRY

My letters seem to me poetry.
Life!
You reconcile me with the all.
Will you always think them poems?
They are *less*, I fear.
I wish my poetry to serve you always.

Madrid 23 January (58) 1933

One of the things I like best is to think
    how the others see you,
how they note in you something has changed.
    You've told me twice.

What is the matter with you?, they ask. Once they
    told you, *You are in love.*
How are you, what's happening, how do you live
    for the rest of them?

I too would like to be those others just to
    see you. Transfigured?
Maybe that's saying much, but I don't believe
    love transfigures us,

Katherine. If you could see how terrified I am
    they will see my face!
It seems to me that everyone will *see you*
    in *my* face. That I wear you

engraved in it as in the soul. Because the secret
    is delicious
as it is sometimes a torment!
    I'm seized by violent fits

not to keep quiet, but to shout it out. Since
    I was in Santander,
on the beach, I have not uttered your name
    aloud. I like to say it

next to the sea or in the great free air.
    I would like you to say
mine when you ride through fields alone
    in your car.

You are name thought, name written,
    but I wish *to say it,*
say it to you. Your name is confirmation
    of your existence,

your identity card. And *to say* your name
      to you is at once having
the reality of you and of your shadow.
      When will I pronounce

your name in your ear? I want to say
      it intimately, right
into your ear after writing it for so long.
      Precisely for being

your name, that others use, that you write
      on envelopes, put on
checks, which for me is unique, distinguished,
      intact. I will invent it

for you, utter it *for the first time* in your ear,
      my life. And then
I'll say it at any time, syllable by syllable
      (and a kiss between

each syllable), letter by letter (and a kiss
      between each letter).

So I'll compensate for the long silence
      of your name, only
written, only thought. Silence, secret, how
      often it weighs on me!

Pedro
Madrid 15 February (72)

YES, I'VE BEEN TO MONTE ESQUINZA, 38

Yes, I've been to Monte Esquinaza, 38.
How can I tell you my impressions?
The first one was in the elevator.
Ugly, old, faded, but consecrated
by you. It took you up many times.
I imagined you alone in the elevator,
in the mornings when you had just

left me at corner, just gone off.
You were still a moment alone
in the elevator. That closed and neutral
room, Katherine, was the place
you had to abandon me, to pull off
the face you made for me and prepare
an indifferent face for greeting C.B.

Not so? Didn't you examine yourself
there in the lift, in the mirror, to see
if there were any perceptible traces
in your appearance of your last feelings?

There in the elevator I dream that you
once said goodbye to me. It was the frontier,
the world's frontier. On entering it
you were still filled with me, but on leaving
for the ordinary world you abandoned
me in that box of wood and glass.

How I dwelled on your quick solitudes
in the lift, on your thoughts about me,
all still heaped together and confused
when we split, a mixture of happiness
and worry that would dominate you
at times! There like lightning you counted.

Pedro
Madrid 16 February (74)

"LOVE, LOVE, CATASTROPHE"

Today they have brought me these proofs
from the printer of my poems to correct.
Reading them I had the live sensation
of depending on you,
of obligation to you, of gratitude,
so I can at least send you them
in this form on bad paper, pure proof,
as it is called, of being nothing.

Because I want you to have this poem
in *all* its forms, that you attend them
in all phases of their life from not being
in manuscript, to proofs, to magazine,
to book. See why? Not literary vanity,
God knows. On seeing them printed,
objectified by the press, removed from me,
I feel them more mine (you know what *mine*
means) than ever. Something ordinary
I have offered you—printer proofs—
but in them I place all the love of

Pedro
Madrid 20 February (76)

PLACE OF ACTION

Place of action. A room in a grand hotel
with its balcony up front. From the balcony
the night is seen. Yes, the night *is seen.* Obscurely,

vaguely, but is seen. And the sea is guessed
a hundred meters off. The reflecting lights
on the ships in the bay signal it. At the foot

of the balcony I have the city, yes,
streetcars, cars, crowds, but I leap over all
that to submerge in the elemental

which lies a bit beyond: night and sea,
a marvelous couple. To come near you
I chose night and sea. The time: seven in

the afternoon. After a fatiguing troubled day.
Rest. I am alone. *Work.* I'm supposed to be
working. The personage: I see him clearly.

In the incoherence of the hotel rooms
a mirror to my right. I see him in the glass.
A tall corpulent man, with two stripes now,

one on the forehead, his face exhausted.
Is it me? I don't like it. No, it's not me.
I am the one writing, the one leaning over

the table, who puts on the paper and in
his pen the best moment of the day. I see
myself, I recognize me, I'm pleased, looking

at me on the leaf of paper, not the sheet
of the looking glass. Because in the mirror
I saw me with my own inevitable marks,

linked to my conditions. But the leaf of
paper doesn't flash back a weary man
but an ageless man, who loves, who is loving

in the full youth of his being. Yes, like that
I'm pleased. I on the paper am I. Freed,
escaping my circumstance with the illusion

of being young, as strong as my love. You
too hold out a mirror to me by loving me.
Love is always a glass that holds the beloved,

a glass not of deforming but purifying,
of elevation, and somehow we see each other
with all pleasure and mirror happiness.

Pedro
[Santander] 30 March (92)

YOU WILL SEE, LIFE. I SHALL HAVE YOUR LETTERS

You will see, life. I shall have your letters
in Paris, it is arranged for the address
and dates I gave you, and you will have mine,

don't worry. Next I want to inform you,
well, *inform* is a bad word, don't know how
to say it: to recognize, thank you, kiss you

for your Boston violet. What a precious tiny
envelope gift you made for me! The label
is an enchantment: "Spring in Boston."

Sentimental, yes, luckily. You recall
what I said one day about the sentimental,
about the cowardly aspiration of the XIX

to tear it out, to amputate it from life,
since it's a *danger,* because it can damage.
Pure cowardice! The odious *Safety first*

of the English, the perfect *slogan* of the
universal bourgeoisie and proletariat,
since workers equally seek security.

Life, always, life, the sentiment with two
knife blades! If it sometimes cuts me too,
so much the better. I'll live in the wound.

Pedro
[Madrid] 12 April (93)

FIRST PARIS WITH YOU!

First Paris with you! I mean with you
in my life, with awareness of your being,
your name, your person! See, I don't have you
now in Paris, only that ideal projection
and yet I have a whole world! I remember
going back to Barcelona, full of wonder,
happiness, mystery, after what happened. Hear
me as one hears a snail shell in which vague

sea noises echo, so I hear in my words
yours and mine, kisses, a recent universe.

Pedro
Paris, 23 April 1933 (94)

THREE BEINGS WE ARE

Three beings we are, Katherine, you said it
a while ago. None of us deserving disgrace
and the three in constant danger of destroying

our lives. And for love, Katherine, for love.
Will we be worthy of this destiny, my soul,
worthy, truly, without diminishing us?

How much you are in my mind! In my mind
at times, maybe spurred on by my fever.
I saw you as a little girl, and in the night

there was a flood and the water rose and rose
and I entered your house and grabbed you
in my arms, asleep, well covered, saved you

and ran off with you, hugging you against me,
filled with joy for liberating you; until far
from the danger I stopped, gazed at you

with infinite love, and you still asleep,
and I thought, where am I taking you now,
where, since I had no house and never, never

wanted to leave you. What would you say
when you awoke? You would say, "Where
are you taking me?" Here my digression ended,

and now, not the girl but you, my love, love
of my soul, seemed to be asking me where
am I taking you to. I don't know if

you might ask, if you have asked without
telling me, Katherine. I tell you: I don't know
where we are going to stop, my love, *but yes,*

blindly, darkly, with a deaf and deep hope
for where I might take you. Is that enough
for living until we arrive? Goodbye, life,

I have written you often. Don't think me
down or hurt, no. These days are the dregs
of my thought. But always, always, yearning

you, love of you, its superiority over
all that has been my light, and my furious dying
to live is always called Katherine and Pedro.

30 January 1934 (106)

THE POEM I SENT YOU YESTERDAY

The poem I sent you yesterday
(and that as I told you I do not consider
definitively finished) made me think
a lot about my poetry, and the state
I'm crossing through because of it.
Will you let me speak of that today?
After our book, its termination and
publication, I have been as one suspended
in poetry, astounded, and wondering,
what's next? The poem seems to be asking me.

You know that I am not *professionally*
a poet. Nothing that I think today,
or my poetry, should be taken as literary,
as professional, and each day less. Among
your many right sayings about our book
is that in it there is not one *clever* line.
There were in my earlier books, many
of my lines were game, dexterity, mental
fun. Nothing more. But in this one, no.
I am happy you see it so clearly, life.

After this book I find myself in a moment
that recalls your recent words, beautiful
and loving, that went from a Sunday picture
to the work itself: I knew that you asked
me for more, much more than I had given.
Not only had I to give myself entirely
but to create more "I." Isn't that it?

These enthralling, moving words got me
to come to a definition of my state,
connecting them to others in the letter
that came later: "You animate me to be
my best I and always incite it to be more."
That's exactly what I feel for my poetry.

Katherine, you know as I do that our book
is the best of mine. I knew it at once.
It would have been a terrible calamity
if these lines composed at the summit of
my life and feeling, written with my full
being were *less* than those I had composed
by the effort of my intelligence and by
the happenstance of transitory intuitions.
I needed to believe in the deep fidelity
of my life and my creation. Clearly, once
there was the color Pedro, that you live.

But, Katherine, not the poem. I never
believed myself capable of writing a poem.
Poetry, yes, a poetic whole as an entity,
but a single work, no. I wrote them with
no intention, with no notion of sequence,
of continuity, of unity. But how they came.

You, Katherine, you, your love gives me
that unity, that tone of faith to feeling,
of living *from* it. You have caused me, not
in my poetry but in all my I, to face life,
look at it straight on, see its profound joy
and its profound tragedy. Through you
my life has found intensity, unknown

dimensions and trembling. Through you I've felt
what there is of eternity, of the immortal.
What is saved in my life, volatile, risky,
perishable. All *revised* by your light.

My feelings and common ways, my friends,
profession, above all an *I*, I have revised,
examined like never before. I found me
through you, for you, deficient, small, incomplete
and sometimes happy. I can say that today
my measure is you. I see me, I analyze me,
I criticize me through you. If I wished I were
younger it is for you; for you I would like
to be younger, more *amiable*, stronger.

You, Katherine, have been, are, the deepest
crisis of my life, the enormous alteration
of my being. Clearly my poetry is part of it.
You have given me, I told you, Katherine,
among other things, *height*. Since I've loved you
my life is *higher*. It has more light, sees more,
feels, like a wind, purer and more difficult.
Height is difficulty, a tower, a campanile,
and harder to live than a stone on the ground.
They have more wind, fight against the laws
of nature. Now, Katherine, my poetry is higher.

Apparent. Not only because I feel it. Everyone
sees it. Even the critics! And *I don't want to
come down*. Katherine, it would be very sad
to descend from that height. I've *tasted* it,
I like its purity, its vital energy, its clarity.
And as you said, soul, it's not enough to give
myself to it entirely; I must create "more I."
And that I can be no other being than what
touches you. I feel my poetry tied indissolubly
to my love, today. I don't say this as a proof
of love, no. If it were not so, if I had other
curiosities and poetic paths, I would not love
you less. The same love has many things that seem
apart from it, but in it they were born.

In all I write and which is not brief or necessarily
intellectual, you, your love, visible or not,
in *poetry of love* or not, you are there.

But for the moment I don't know how to write
or write but what I have written these two years.
Love poetry is what comes out of me. Now
my anxiety is that it doesn't make the rest
unworthy, which might be another expanded
Voice Because of You, within a year. I'm waiting
for *me* poetically as I wait for *you* in my life.

I don't know. I *project* nothing, I propose nothing,
but I believe and wait. As you see my soul attitude
is the same as for my most intimate life.
I believe in what will come. I am preparing it
and preparing me for it, deaf, slowly, as one
prepares in the earth a desire to live. So I am
astonished, halted, to see what comes out,
and any time something comes and I send it
to you, I hope to see me in you. Because
the lines of this year no one knows like you,
no one; I have read them to no one, not out
of desire that they be unknown. No, because
I don't *need* it, because they are my happy lines,
and in your reading them they already live
their most faithful life and they are fulfilled.

Your Pedro
Madrid 20 March 1934 (113)

I AM IN THE TRAIN

I am in the train. Even worse handwriting!
Poor little one! Will you stop loving me
because of penmanship? When two who love

are separated, heaven should at least
concede them a good hand. It has for you,
not me. Two hours ago I wrote you from

the terrace of the Magdalena. Now
I keep writing. Pure fidelity to myself;
I do what *solely* I can do. In this site,

a train compartment, alone, at this hour,
at seven, the day ending. I *can't* do anything
else. The two hundred pieces of business

to do in Santander are erased from my head.
I live for myself. I enjoy the unparalleled
felicity this solitude accompanied

by a moving landscape, this quick and casual
solitude where you follow me. Because now
there is not solitude for me. The one possible

solitude today is that you do not love me.
How I've been caught up, Katherine, in our love
these last two days! I stayed alone in Santander,

lovely weather, I felt a kind of unanticipated
and delicious vacation. I spent long periods
nest to the sea. Some minutes on the beach

(there I read your letters from Boston) I wrote
lines. The good Pedro, still alive, awoke
in me, he who contemplates, dreams and hopes.

I was pleased to feel him. I haven't died
under the weight of the businessman. I
recognize him. He is the same one who

in Madrid exists only one hour a day when
he writes letters to the one you know.
And what was I to dream, to contemplate

but my Katherine and my love? These are not
happy days in the common sense of the world.
I want to explain what has happened. I hope

I can do it in a hand you can decipher.
These have been days of spiritual withdrawal,
of self-appraisal. I love you, Katherine, a lot.

But I don't carry your love lightly, as something
sure and positive and taken for granted.
No. I want my love always to be aware

of the miracle, the wonder, the uniqueness.
I want to see it not in plain illumination,
as a habit of your life, but lighted by chance,

astonishment that brings us to life. Get it?
I don't want to discard the fundamentals
of love, its ways, difficulties, abandonments.

I like to return slowly over them as one opens
a box with loved objects and take them out
and stare at them slowly, caress them, and

drop them, brimming with happiness with the
conviction that they are precious as we thought,
so I open a window on our love, which I've

gone over and over with infinite emotion.
The past, the present, the future I look at
in relation to you. One can say all of me

is a relation with you, below your sign.
I don't hide anything. The irreparable
of a past without you, of your past without

me that have anguished me for these two days.
The hardship of the present, without risks,
the patience and spiritual heroism you need

to love me, my situation, all I've seen again.
For the future I ask only one condition.
Not that it be short or long, live a lot

or little, I don't ask it to be happy or desolate.
I ask only that *it be with your love*. The future
can be of only two ways: your loving me

or your not loving me. That's it, Katherine,
yesterday, today, tomorrow have moved on
slowly like the color of the sea green, blue,

and at times gray . . . .

In the train 4 of April 1935 (115)

HOW TERRIBLE THE SUNDAYS ARE!

How terrible the Sundays are, Katherine!
Recollection intensifies and sharpens
in a huge way. These were days so much ours!

Living embrace! Never is that perfect state
felt wider than Sundays. Pure embrace, Sunday,
Katherine. The nostalgia of my whole surrender

to you, my whole possession of you, at night,
in dream, kiss, morning, kiss, waking, kiss,
endlessly, the Sundays encircle me

like never before. The marvel of your body
beside me, all night, to live naturally,
sleeping, next to me, lying in wait for

your waking, my wait to catch the first ray
of your eyes, the first sound of your voice,
the first hunger to kiss your lips, first love

of your soul, in the new day, all a treasure
of my memory and desire to return
in my soul and body. Oh, Katherine,

that it be true! That I might live hugging you,
always! That what might be true again what
was so beautiful. *It must be.* To live embracing,

Katherine. Only with that body and that soul
that has your name and my love can I live
in embracing arms. I don't want other arms,

now. Either yours or solitude. But my loneliness
waits for you, thirsts for you, desires you,
all my life. I have a weird sensation. Since

my bodily I is quiet in its place, doesn't go
to you, my soul never stops walking, pacing
in search of you. I feel my soul, hear its steps

incessantly toward you, and it never stops
a second. It seeks you. I seek you, Katherine,
I seek you for what you have given me

and what I hope from you, I seek with re-
cognition, and ineffable joy for those days
of living in our arms and a thirst and longing

and illusion of our once again in each other's
arms. Pardon, Katherine, if I seem a bit passionate
to you, but it is my mood after a Sunday.

Pedro
Madrid 23 March 1936 (121)

KATHERINE OF MY SOUL

Katherine of my soul, you have written me
a letter about that Sunday afternoon you spent

reading our poetry, for which I thank you.
Maybe if you could have perceived the flood

of spiritual pleasure, of love's joy, my soul
won as it read. That's the best way of telling

my thanks. You filled me with light, love. You filled
me with equipoise for all. Because here

in this terrain is where two hearts can make
a date always without fear of anything.

Our poetry is like our home unconquerable
by anyone, our private paradise, the space

that we have earned to create ourselves, forever.
I have not said it to you more, for it always

makes me pause (for seeming to be the author's
vanity—poor thing!), but I ask you whenever

you feel doubts or torments in the soul, or
if I have not behaved well with you, come

to our poetry, and I am sure that there
we will find ourselves, with no mist or pain.

If in something I have on a day failed you,
maybe you can forgive me through that poetry.

If you find I've not done for you what I should have,
that can serve as a reason for pardon. Since

it is a distinctive label of our love, which makes it
unique in my life and I believe in yours.

Let us never abandon it, soul. I beg
you wherever you go, carry our book.

This year, commenting in a class on Garcilaso
and Bécquer, you can't know how many times

I thought (modestly, yes, as to the literary,
but proud as to the human) in the beautiful

of our secret destiny. How happy I am
to owe my best poetry not to me, not

to my individual invention, but to your
inspiring collaboration! I shall never be

alone in my poetry. I'll turn my eyes to you.
And you might turn to yourself, see yourself

and think that those eyes have caused to be
born what without you would never have

had birth. A while ago I was reading the new
Historia de la literature española by Valbuena.

And on reading this: "*La voz a ti debida*
is the great contemporary poem of love,

of complete unity of love," I assure you
that I did not feel the least vain flattery,

but I turned my soul to you, saying: "I hope
it's true for HER." I know whatever happens

I can't be *one* in your life among others,
but something a little more, because you

will always be joined to me for a something
that cannot join you to anyone else.

Your Pedro
Wellesley, Friday night 3 of June 1938 (130)

[Katherine is in Mexico]

MEXICO IS FOR ME

Mexico is for me an uninterrupted chain
of emotions. Everything speaks to me here.
It is many years since a city has caught me
as so profound and rich in diversity.
I am living in a state of constant *acquisition.*
You can't imagine what it is. Everywhere
memories of Spain leap to my eyes, my ears,
my smell, my soul. It's a living again;

it is a "rencontre du temps perdu," as Proust
would say. I'm enthralled to live in what was,
because this city not only carries me through space,
from here to my country, but also in time.
From my present state to my childhood.

It represents in many things a form of older
Spanish life of twenty or thirty years ago.
In streets around the *Catedral* I dream
I am stepping through the boy I was.
On entering the Church I spotted a lady
dressed exactly, with her veil and dark dress,
like mother. The movement in the streets,
the voices of the people, all, being today
and present, seems to come for me from
my childhood. The most puzzling is I don't see
specific parts of Spain but something from all,
mixed. Mexico is a synthesis of the Spanish:
not Andalusian nor Castilian, no Levantine
in a pure state but a subtle combination
of several themes. And I go on with my *eager
heartedness* reborn, those themes, the same
as could appear in a musical work. I enjoy
the ineffable, from those *nadas,* from those
reminiscences of what I was and what I see.

The impression is very strange and lovely.
Nothing of that had I seen. It comes before
my eyes for the first time. Yet I had seen all,
all was in me. A curious sensation of deep
familiarity and apparent strangeness. Exquisite.
You will understand that this same emotion
for its depth and intensity takes me
on an indirect road to you. Because what immense
happiness for me to have been able to feel
such intimate and new things at your side,
to relive the ancient of my life next to
its newest, your love! I do not know how
to feel alone, I do not want to feel alone.
And with no one but with you would I feel

all this. I am sure you would know it better
if you were here now, right here at my side.

Pedro
Mexico City, Monday 29 of August 1938 (132)

MY KATHERINE

My Katherine, the joy your Monday letter
brought me can be compared to gusts of wind
from sea or land that envelop you, caress you,

toning the flesh and soul all at once. Reading it
I felt a new force rising in me, from you,
beautiful like a force of nature. I could not

be wrong. Though in with different words
and ways we were saying the same in our two letters
that had crossed after the day in New York.

It couldn't have been otherwise. What a disaster
if either of us had stopped feeling and understanding
all the new richness and clarity we reached!

Katherine, jubilance, jubilance, happiness
because we have lived and felt in unison,
because you came happy to me and I came

full of pleasure and glory from you. I suppose
my letter gave you tranquility also;
perhaps you feared that separating from me

completely satisfactory; and you have seen,
soul, that you gave me a multitude of love
like no other, though you have given me

the most beautiful ones. These two letters
have been like an embrace. Two arms open
at the same instant in an absolute coincidence
of wanting to hug each with the same greed.

What dexterity, yes. Your shadows and mine
asked for realities, like earlier, now. The day
in New York gave them to us in a complete

and delicate way. Seeing each other again
gave body to all that in these months demanded
of a body. And giving body to our shadows,

and not just more corporeal and material
but more subtle and spiritual. Thank you,
my soul, for having converted your pleasure
of a Sunday into the finest act of love.

Pedro
Wellesley Friday 11 of November 1938 (138)

FOR THE REST I SEE TODAY

For the rest I see today already outside of us,
and my general life. I can't feel less than
deeply grateful before hazard. I lost my house,
many things in it were precious to me. I lost

my career and my social position in Spain.
My poor fortune perhaps has disappeared.
All those losses are on a scale. In another
column are many, many things. I've found

a decent professional position that lets me
live. Above all I've found a site, a country
where I can be. I am not an *outcast*. America
is not for me exile where by obligation and

distaste I survive. No. America is generous
and good, and I am surrounded by a lovely
and serene ambience. But it is difficult,
Katherine, living with pleasure in a foreign land.

There are things rooted down in my being,
which at my age call me to the homeland.
Yet I live pleased here. So as time passes, rather
than inciting a feeling of strangeness in

the foreign, it strengthens my fondness for this nation,
and a desire to become part of it where possible
and discreet. I am happy, Katherine, because I see
my spirit is still not closed down, frozen and stiff,

which tends to happen with the years. It is
open to the new, wanting more, to understand.
I expect hard tests, especially as to my literary
profession. That is what naturally I cannot ask

America: an audience, a climate for my poetry.
But no matter. I will find a way out of all this.
What is essential is the spiritual lean, the *anima*.
With a good anima, feeling oneself animated,

everything surging forth will be easy to solve.
I swear to you, my love, that in these days
I feel great anima, wanting to live and to make
others live. So I can't feel less than gratitude,

for the *urge to be alive*. All this is transparent
when I consider the particular life
I have found, while away from it the horror
and tragedy of my country goes on in hot blood.

On that front there is no peace, no satisfaction,
no tranquility. Just the opposite. But even that,
the collective whole, it is best to confront
with a courageous rather than a weak anima.

I know they will not rob me of *my* Spain,
the one I carry in me since I was born,
which is only mine, which I will defend
down through the profundities of my soul.

And something else. With every passing day
I feel more faith in the force of the singular
person. The social is concerned only with material
and common things of life, but the beautiful

and great, the delicate is shaped and born
in the secret of souls and human beings.
While I have come to a huge disillusion
and absolute scorn for the forms and use

of political life in general and of a man
as a political being; and while I lost Europe
and have lost faith in many collective schemes
I embrace faith in souls, in good smart beings,

and love. So I have, my Katherine, *reasons
for living*, for moving on; and if a rain
of bitterness falls on me at times when

I look on human ignominies, I turn
to everlasting beauty which is the spark
igniting the soul, and that is the only

source for living. I need not say that you
have made my state today. Behind motions
of soul, partly visible, are you. You are

the grand *reason for which I live* with anima
and faith. Nothing else, my precious one.
You wrote me a congratulations letter
and I a letter of recognition and thanks.

All else is external and for another day
when I receive another letter from you.
Your Pedro, one year older, offers you love
and a life that wants to be a lot younger. Your

Pedro
Wellesley 27 of November 1938 Sunday (139)

We are hemmed in by snow. How wondrous
to gaze at it! How white, smooth, how pure

is seems! I look at it and my spirit changes:
a species of gentleness of soul, amplitude

of vision invades me. In this snow so intact,
so clean, there is no evil, no pain, no anguish.

She does not suffer or cause suffering.
It has no memory, no hopes, no intentions.

It is as it is, elemental, paradisiacal, before
good was born, before evil, consciousness,

people. Seeing it I feel what I felt when writing
some poems of *My Voice,* the poems of pure

and happy love. Across the snow, imperfections
and inequalities are erased, all appears simple

and one. Better than reading, than thinking;
this afternoon is gazing, gazing at snow,

holding its soul, reclining in its whiteness
as in a death without death, without suffering,

as on a shoulder, as on a loved being or on
a life. Perhaps you remember something

in these words! Some nights or days when
I too reclined in just this way, Katherine.

Your
Pedro
Wellesley Monday [March?]1939 (142)

Don't think I am afraid to see each other
in Springfield for abstract reasons. No.
I was in the train restaurant a month

and a half ago on the Sunday train
and when it stopped in Springfield I saw
two people waving at me from the platform:

Justa Arroyo and Susana Fitzgerald.
I got off a moment to speak with them.
I understood that Justa is running loose

all about here, like a *traffic cop*. I'm not
afraid, no. I overhear in your letter
the sound of a note of *disappointment*

over this. But—at least I believe this sincerely—
it's not fear. It's something that occurs
in the mind, to walk on tiptoes, with high

care not to feel the weight of the earth
at each step. It is like an indispensable
delicacy because everything is delicate

and subtle today. I adore you through
a thinnest veil of gauze, behind which
we see each other a bit like shadows,

and though the material is not consistent
to prevent us from touching, it is respected
by both of us as if it were. This cloth

creates a phantasmagorical world
where relations of time, reality, distance
are not the same. I haven't changed, no.

But in me I carry *another I,* Katherine.
And this other I seizes my arm when
I am about to leap to you. It shuts

my mouth when I am about *to say the word*
that can't be said; it puts its hand on my eyes
when in them it sees the old flame. This other

I stands before you and smiles to you with clarity
as if a brother of mine. I don't know whether
all this *makes any sense for you*. I feel it in me.

The coming days will be very uncertain
as you know. I had planned to spend eight
or ten days in New York, on vacation,

and we might have seen each other. Now
I know nothing. All depends on the operation.
If, as I hope, Margarita comes out well

and comes back home around the 28th,
I would be in New York four days, from
the 3rd to the 7th, more or less. Goodbye,

Katherine, my dearest one.

Pedro
Wellesley Monday 11 of December 1939 (146)

KATHERINE OF MY SOUL, I WRITE THESE WORDS

Katherine of my soul, I write these words
and it seems a lie. Again writing to you.

Again looking for you, not in high silence
in the absence of all word as so often

I have done in the past, but in truth,
in divine *correspondence!* Perhaps you think

I've not been quick in answering you,
life. Nothing like that. But one of those stupid

incidents happened. Your letter got here
before I did. And a foolish employee

sent it to the department with other mail.
And there that packet of letters lay sleeping

till today. I'm going crazy over the ineptitude
of the Club Manager. Not for the other letters,

that were not important, but this one, yours
which I picked up, opened and read, almost

in a spasm. So I answer you the same day
that I get it, despite the delay. Not mine, no.

How could I delay in something that my heart
is begging, desiring (and unable to tell

you anything) for months and for months?
I don't know how it has been for you, in

you, your soul, these months of forced
silence. For me they have not been lost.

A proof. A proof harder than any, proof
of silence, of not knowing, of being like

lost in the same world without the probability
of finding us. Nevertheless, I have not doubted

our love. How can a silence of today, of months,
end with something like what we create? Maybe

we don't matter much now. I don't ask you
if you love me, nor do I tell you if I love you.

No the *eager hearted* Pedro, as you called me,
I the great unruly asker don't ask. I who

have told you in a million ways, who've written
you in a million ways, I don't write it now.

But I said it, you said it, we said it to
each other, and those two voices will never

be silenced, never. I surmise that your voice
when you said you loved me, and mine when I said

it to you, are today in a kind of heaven
or paradise, saved from mortality,

and above us. I like to think us joined
like a cascade in which two currents of water

coincide, and which does not stop falling
and speaking its speech. Perhaps we value

less what we say than what we create. Maybe
we, our beings are solely material like

a sculptor's stone, the painter's color, with
which one chosen day we manage to create

beauty, elevating us from our un-formation
to a plenitude in exquisite form.

Yes, my soul. I look at you in my thought,
and I swear I find no reproach in me,

nor desperation, nor bitterness, and scarcely
pain. To you goes my heart with infinite

gratitude, with indelible memory
of joy and life; it goes to you as toward

a unique happening in the world, distinct
from all the rest, alone, in the solitude

of incomparable beauty. Because in you
my life took on an aspect it never had

earlier in my eyes, for mind and whole being.
If I have called you a thousand times "my life,"

it is because you were the corporeal way,
the reduction to a human form of beauty

itself in life. Torpid my love, but what bright
vision of you! So, Katherine, how can I see you

today but with the same sense of miracle,
of marvel, of spell, as I received you

when you came? Why will the months, the years
of obstacles, of worries, of vexations

wipe out the timeless, the hours, the minutes
in which my life was much more than time,

was incalculable, incapable of being reduced
to measure, infinite as your love made it?

My ordinary life is made of clock time—
so I count and measure it. But my highest life

released from normal rule, was made of
eternity. So I am older, I've lost much,

I look at myself with pain. But that life
of mine I created by your side resides in

its eternity, has not followed my pettiness
and weaknesses. It is no longer mine

in terms of possession. It is itself
risen to immortality. Maybe you won't

see it again. I don't care to see you
as the last time in Boston. Yet I'll never

stop seeing you. For I need it. Seeing you
in soul and memory is seeing the highest

of myself. Seeing you inside me is to see
the most complete and luminous life that chance

gave me. So I go on seeing without you
seeing me, nor hearing me, because I need

to feel and know what was the peak
of my existence, once, in one timeless day.
Today I hope that there may come to you
only one clarity of me. A clarity like the

serene and quiet one between a beautiful
day and a beautiful night, and which holds

more light than the sun or moon. Your

Pedro
Faculty Club
Berkeley 7 of July 1941 (148)

NO, THIS TIME I WON'T LET TIME FLY

No, this time I won't let time fly.
I got your letter this morning. Here

I am same night at the machine,
as so many times, my thoughts on you.

What a weird unpredictable life!
I write you so often full of anxiety

of immediate ardor, hoping to see you,
and now I have a *celestial* serenity;

I suppose what clouds must feel skimming
over the earth, over their beauties,

A lofty pleasure, remote; they know
they can never again come near

those handsome realities seen
below. Yet they're content in floating

over them as a pure goal for their
glances. Where are you, for me, today?

In the past? No. Nor in the present
or future. You are in timeless time,

in some kind of eternity of life.
Before, in the period of my human love

(too human!) I saw you through days,
months, years. I calculated: "I must wait

this long to see her! It's so long
since I've seen her." I lived the anguish

of time. Today the bars of that cage
are broken. Can make no calculation.

I float over your absence, not quickly
or slow, outside of computation.

Now you are wholly incalculable.
You are beyond mistakes in counting.

I can't think now of ciphers as
to when and for how long I'll see

you. How I would plead for hours,
minutes, a tiny bit more of time!

Do you remember? I've no regret.
I did well. Those hours and minutes

are so rich that to have had them
is the essence of my life. Now

I don't dream of asking, not even
to myself. Free of numbers, my

Katherine. Sometimes I'm afraid
to see you like this. It is too

immortal, too much eternity.
Seems like you are no longer alive

but in an afterlife. Really
neither you nor I live in this world.

Then? Maybe so, the cloud, the in-
calculable, the afterlife, in

another world where we have arrived.
The only possible one. The one

beating in my heart like an omen,
an unforgettable night in Barcelona,

when before returning to the Hotel,
the first year, we were scouting

through the street all the houses, and
all the doors were locked and we laughed,

and in our depths an anxiety.
Luckily, for the rest you live

solidly in this world. I too.
I'm the only one who takes you

out of this world, as you do for
me. From time to time we go

from our arms to aerial spheres
while we go on apparently

in this world. No one notices.
We continue there materially,

the others see us. But I make dates
nameless and numberless. You come

and we have a crazy wild time
through immense spaces, till I think

at times that other world, the other,
is this one. May the date be true.

May the arm that is your marvelous
arm be true. But we let out the

great shout: *Viva* the wind! And
The solitary truth from wind.

Katherine, I've three weeks left
here. Write me, since later on . . . !

Suddenly I feel like crying. But that
is of *this* world. *Viva* the wind!

Pedro
Berkeley July 1941 (149)

HOW CAN I TELL YOU MY EMOTION!

How can I tell you my emotion on getting
your letter! Of *foreboding,* a presentiment
that would seem to be mere superstition
and this time real. It was only an envelope,
typed, and I felt the inexplicable passion,
with your idea, with your image, with your name,
Katherine, an emotion from you, solely
possible from you! Your letter, so good,
generous, filled me with thought and deep
and silenced happiness. What could you have thought
of me? How often I've thought precisely
about that, about what you would think of me.

Your love, your good heart is what I see;
let my behavior, my inexplicable silence, yes,
inexplicable in keeping with appearances,
not make you think me as bad as it deserves.
Yet the explanation, Katherine, is simple, vulgar!
One sole word: the censor. I wrote you from
the hotel in Miami some hurried lines, assuring
you of my love, of my remembrance. And here
I am. And before writing you, a scandalous letter
in the press: a professor who informed her college
in America about a Puerto Rican candidate

for a position there, unfavorable moral reasons.
Then the person accused shows up at the professor's
house, assaults her, punches her out. A big
struggle. How was it known what was said
in the letter? Then it came out that a clerk
in the censor, a friend of the candidate,
had make a copy of the letter. I realized
at once that in the offices of the censor
were a bunch of irresponsible and gossiping
girls who liked to go through personal letters
and then divulge their contents to their friends.
I was hardly here a few weeks when I understood
the impassable obstacle that was the censor.

I got to know people who were working there,
not the gossipers, but even they knew who
had written you. I don't know if you can imagine
the absurd situation. To write you was to risk
all kinds of terrible unpleasantness,
at any moment. This city is small, everyone
knows each other and when a foreigner comes
like me, he is the object of public attention.

A letter was to test an unfathomable outcome,
Katherine. You can't imagine my doubts,
what I fought, what I went through. In moments
I most needed your friendly words, reason,
recollection, memory, consolation, company!
When I most wanted to help you in your pain!
There was no way. Once I had the sensation
of escaping danger of entering into the game
of censorship. I went to Cuba in 1944, sent
some lines which I suppose you received. Yet
I still couldn't explain anything, since the office
of the Miami bureau had the same people as
from here. For months, Katherine, I felt trapped,
bound by an invisible force, superior to me.
Then came habit, terrible habit. But how much
I dote on you in what you think is my silence.
. . . .
Katherine, now you don't write me yet. I will
keep writing you, if you let me. I have many,

many things to recount! It makes me so happy
to be able to communicate with you, to free
my soul, to let the words flow as before!
Let me write you. I shall do it right away.
Don't take that joy from me! I'll tell you when
and how you can reach me. Do you understand,
really? I say only one thing more to you:
thanks and thanks and thanks. I hope you'll find
all you deserve through your generosity
of soul. I am . . . what you might love.

Pedro
San Juan, Puerto Rico 9 February 1946 (150)

I AM DELIGHTED, DEAREST KATHERINE

I am delighted, dearest Katherine,
that next year you are going abroad.

You have earned it after these past
years of suffering. Don't know what

to tell you about your trip. In Spain
you'll find a painful and miserable

material life around you. Though you
will lack nothing, it may be hurtful

to live in the midst of privations.
An impoverished intellectual life,

almost reduced to nothing. The Center
a farce, University, only in name.

Of course you can do your own work.
That yes. At the same time you might be

better off in South America,
though the intellectual life has no great

revelation except in Buenos Aires
and now Perón is trashing that.

In Washington a few brief hours, what
can I say? Your words might be mine.

But what words do I have the right
to pronounce today, thinking of

you? What I might feel, what I am
feeling, here it is and no reason

to kill it off. But its expression,
especially directed to you,

helps nothing. You have *seen*. That is
what's important. You have seen me

in speech, my face, in all there is
in me. I also have seen, Katherine,

all in you, all I always saw,
and about that, sufferings, pains, in which

I have my role, without wanting to.

You and I have participated
in greatest happiness and great

pain. But in that pain I could not
accompany you as I would have

wished to. I feel in debt and at fault,
not wanting it, ever. Our companion-

ship is stranger and more complex
than ever. Made worse by my life

circumstance. Sometimes I think
that our love and we are distinct,

that we are walking on one side,
it on the other. But of its existence

I don't doubt, after having seen you
and wanting to see you more, much more.

But so rare is that sensation that
I have delayed more than I cared to

in writing you. Do you understand?
Forgive always your

Pedro
Baltimore, autumn? 1947 (151)

Pedro Salinas, Middlebury, Vermont (ca. 1951). Courtesy the Heirs of Pedro Salinas.

Pedro Salinas: Between the Old and the New

Pedro Salinas was a leading figure in Spain's literary scene in the years before the civil war. Among his most significant achievements one can mention his prolific activities as a literature professor, poet, short story writer, novelist, dramatist, and essayist. He was also a literary critic with an unrivaled dedication to the art of letter writing, and founder of the Universidad Internacional in Santander (1933–36). He was both witness to and an active participant of the II Spanish Republic of 1931. Like no other poet of his group (the so-called Generation of 1927), he was able to excel in many different fields, while pursuing an intellectual and administrative career. But like many others he also fell prey to the militarist brutality of the era and decided to go into exile.

As a witness to a world in uproar, in America Salinas discovered and wholeheartedly explored a radically distinct reality that he recorded with his always sharp and intricately thoughtful pen. The books and letters he wrote at Wellesley College and at Johns Hopkins, or while traveling through the United States and the Americas, not only capture the profound social transformations in, for him, the new continents, but paint a revelatory portrait of the author himself. Here we have a recently escaped inhabitant of artistically vital but chaotic old-world Madrid, suddenly on his own as a literary exile in the New World. Possessing a Borgesean memory, a few books, elementary English, and an indomitable literary imagination, Salinas threw himself into poems, plays, fiction, and a multitude of letters. These writings shrewdly document the zeitgeist of the isolated but outstanding Spanish artist-intellectual who spent his exile among several fine American universities. The *republicanos*, exiles from democratic Spain like Salinas, had the singular duty of recreating their oeuvre and their lives, while keeping alive a Spain that was, and that was now being transformed into the vengeful fascist regime of Generalísimo Francisco Franco, Cacique of Spain by the grace of God. In these refugees we have a panoply of renascent pre-war Spain, including Tomás Navarro Tomás and Jorge Guillén in the States, Juan Ramón Jiménez in Puerto Rico, Luis Cernuda and Luis Buñuel in Mexico, and Rafael

Alberti and José Ortega y Gasset in Argentina. They did not dry up any more than Chopin did in fleeing occupied Poland or Joyce in escaping religion-heavy Ireland. Indeed, the concordant and enormous artistic production of these decades represents a universalizing triumph of the last Spanish diaspora.

*

The Spanish essayist and philosopher María Zambrano speaks of the 1920s and '30s as a defining moment in Spanish culture, a "historical moment," a staggering crossroad of transformations, a peak period of intense literary and artistic renovation. She called it a "Silver Age" in Spanish culture—the sequel to the sixteenth- and seventeenth-century "Golden Age" of John of the Cross, Greco, and Cervantes. This fertile new period was abruptly interrupted by the civil war. In poetry, the vindication of a series of forgotten classical figures (Góngora and Garcilaso) occurred, along with more contemporary writers (such as Gustavo Bécquer, Rubén Darío, and Juan Ramón Jiménez) who were echoes in the formation of the new poetic voices. The older *modernista* poets professed artistic purity and melodic poetic form, but the next generation, that of the '27 authors, needed more than the exquisite, the French in Spanish dress. They were an avant-garde. With great dexterity they also experimented with form, old and new, and they looked to the experimental Mallarmean "Book" as a way to organize their poetry. Federico García Lorca, Rafael Alberti, and Miguel Hernández were imbued with medieval popular song and ballad, the *poesía* popular of Andalusia and Castille. Salinas and Jorge Guillén, among others, wrote luminous intellectual constructs where everyday life shone under new light. Vicente Aleixandre and Luis Cernuda, the Alexandrian Cavafys of their day, transformed a world of secluded ignominious love into an astonishing, subjugated nature-based imagery. All the poets indulged in a vindication of new images. Ortega wrote, "Today's poetry is the superior algebra of metaphors."[1] They were into intemporality and aesthetic transcendence. So they were many and with many forms of freshness: universality and cosmopolitanism, popular and traditional poetry, and by the 1930s surrealism and engaged literature. The civil war, the huge uprooting, and its aftermath changed everything.

The 1920s in Spain saw a diffusion of new poetical attitudes through anthologies, manifestos, journals, and publishing houses. The celebration of Góngora's centennial in 1927 signified a moment of strength for a

1. José Ortega y Gasset, *La deshumanización del arte* (Madrid: Revista de Occidente, 1925).

group of young writers, and this moment defined enduring friendships, even some with few literary affinities. No matter: the mood was one of great enthusiasm for art. But with the coming of the 1936–39 war and WWII, everything came to a dramatic halt. The options were life and art under dictatorship or in exile. But in Pedro Salinas we have old Spain and the itinerant wanderer of what was, during the colonial period called *La Nueva España* (the new Spain).

*

Willis Barnstone is a fine translator and reader of poetry. His rendition of Salinas's letters as poems is truly a wonderful achievement. He has discerned poems contained in the letters and he has been able to render them as such. His feat stresses both the poet Barnstone's facility to recognize poems concealed in Salinas's prose letters, and also his ability to deal in a sophisticated, original way with the inferences of love. But in doing so, Barnstone reminds us of the way the Spanish author, who has been encapsulated for posterity as a poet, pioneered innovative ways of expression and inquiry into human feelings. And Pedro Salinas was more than the poet of love, "the deepest human adventure," as Barnstone puts it; in his work he went beyond providing lines and quotes for speechless lovers in need of speech. To read Pedro Salinas's work under the limited light of twentieth-century love poetry, no matter what the depth and sophistication of his achievements, is a disservice to his reputation. Salinas, a modern intellectual, first in Spain and later in the United States, took a complex and contradictory way as he floated off in the uplifting word.

To broaden the perspective on Salinas—beyond his skilful and innovative mastery of love poetry—allows the reader to perceive a modern intellectual who grew up and lived for years in a landscape of provincial limitations set by the Spanish society of the early twentieth century. Indeed, he was a leader in a group of intellectuals who set higher standards for their country. Aiming at modernity, he fought against the conservative mood, against the Iberian caveman mentality. In favor of radical change, Salinas wrote most of his literary work against all odds. But he would pursue a dual objective. Like Rilke's *Angelus Novus* (angel of history), he looked backward without forgetting about the past while walking forward toward the future. Salinas is fascinated with the wonders of modernity. In a playful way, he incorporated this interest into his work. In a sort of fatal attraction toward machinery and artifacts, he wrote splendid poems, such as the one devoted to "Underwood girls." He perceives the letters of a typewriter as a chorus line dancing in front of the writer when doing his work. Having lived in Paris from 1912 to 1915, Salinas was aware, long before other Spanish writers, of the avant-gardes and their radical aesthetics. One of his impressions of Paris reflects his dual attitude: "Es hermoso, esto. Es como todo París, tradición y modernidad, raíz y hoja fresca." (This is beautiful. It is like everything in Paris, tradition and modernity, roots and new leaves.)[2]

When he was exiled in the United States, he was surprised in a positive way by New York's gruesome aspect. The poetic rendering of his impressions are a variation on Federico García Lorca's reaction in *Poet in New York* (1929), or Julio Camba's depiction as "ciudad automática" (automated city) (1930). Salinas perceived the city's gloomy modernity as a sign of a different civilization, one marked by machines and intense solitude, a solitude in a forest of skyscrapers that he had envisioned in one of his best avant-garde prose pieces, "Entrada en Sevilla" (Entry into Seville), which describes an aerial vision from within a space in the threshold of transformation from town to city. A letter from 1935 expresses his fascination with the new experiences offered by Modernity, and reflects an attitude that he never abandoned. In the letter, in which he describes traveling by car at night from Madrid to Guadarrama as he listens to the radio, a concert broadcast from a distant central European concert hall, and encounters the flashing lights from other cars, Salinas expresses his happiness at "the new."[3] His characteristic "desire for clarity" can be traced in *Todo más claro* (Everything clearer) (1949), a set of long poems devoted to the encounter between a city of the mind, one that he recognizes in nature, on the one hand, and in Modernity, on the other. Yet, while he embraced the positive changes of a new technological age, he was also aware of its unprecedented danger. Extremely pessimistic in tone, he devotes an entire section, "Cero" (Zero), to the fear of the atomic bomb. Reflecting this mixed attitude of attraction and alarm toward modernity in other poems in the same collection, he refers to New York's electric billboards as some sort of new constellation of stars.

Salinas had a contradictory outlook representative of a changing worldview: he was in favor (but with some reservations) of Modernity, its new, city-centered world, its bourgeois attitudes and rationalist implications. He was torn between life's variety and the difficulty to grasp it in calculated terms; he was convinced of the need for rationality as a way of controlling nature. As a traveler, lover, writer, and professor, he always expressed this unfathomable contradiction. His life was determined

2. Pedro Salinas, *Epistolario Completo. Obras Completas III*, edited by Enric Bou and Andrés Soria Olmedo (Madrid: Cátedra, 2007), 105.

3. Ibid., 473–74.

by his curiosity. Thus his intimate friend Jorge Guillén defined him in these words:

> Salinas, que conocía muy bien las alturas supremas, era un incesante Colón de Indias anónimas, de esos aciertos que la vida no catalogada propone al desgaire en este o el otro minuto.

. . .

> Salinas, who knew high culture very well, was an incessant Columbus of the anonymous Indies, of those surprises that non-catalogued life provides inadvertently at any moment.[4]

Salinas lamented on many occasions his situation as a Spanish exile in an English-speaking country. He complained particularly about the irony of writing theater and not being able to see it performed:

> Aquí estoy *lejos de todo*: el mundo literario y teatral me es desconocido. . . . En España mi nombre literario me abría todas las puertas; aquí no tengo nombre, sino entre unos pocos enterados de lo español.

. . .

> Here I am *far from everything*: the literary or theater world is unknown to me. . . . In Spain my literary name would open any door; here I do not have a name, except for a few people familiar with Spanish literature.[5]

He lived a desperate situation. After arriving in Wellesley in 1936, he wrote fourteen plays, of which he only saw one performed, a few months before his death, by a group of Barnard College students. In his lifetime, Salinas experienced frustration in not finding an audience for his literary production in the United States because of the lack of translations. The only exceptions would be the volume of essays *Reality and the Poet in Spanish Poetry*, which was the result of the 1937 Turnbull lectures at Johns Hopkins University; and three anthologies of his poetry, translated by Eleanor Turnbull: *Lost Angel and Other Poems* (1938), *Truth of Two and Other Poems* (1940), and *Sea of San Juan: A Contemplation* (1950). A shrewd literary critic in newspapers and in the Centro de Estudios Históricos (Center for historical studies) before the war, he devoted considerable attention

---

4. Jorge Guillén, "Elogio De Pedro Salinas," in *Pedro Salinas*, ed. Andrew Debicki (Madrid: Editorial Taurus, 1976), 31.

5. Salinas, *Epistolario Completo*, 570.

to the emerging poets of his time (Alberti and Aleixandre, among others). In the United States, his essays in *El defensor* (The defender) (1947) are sharp inquiries into topics of the time: language, letter writing, and readership.

*

Willis Barnstone's discovery of the poems hiding in Salinas's letters to Katherine Whitmore points to the importance that letter writing held for Salinas in life and in his writings, in theory *and* in practice. The third volume of the recent 2007 edition of Salinas's complete works contains a selection of a mere thousand letters, the tip of the iceberg of a strenuous, lifetime activity. Letters are like diaries (as noted by Maurice Blanchot); they are glimpses of future books, crucial annotated information about the *work in progress*. In Salinas's case, it is the kind of writing that allows the reader to witness, according to Claudio Guillén, Salinas's "multiplicity."[6] Through the letters, one discovers the dimensions of Salinas's "debts" of affection to friends and family, his "atenciones" (attentions), as Jorge Guillén says. But at the same time the letters offer a glimpse into Salinas's honesty as a writer. His radicalism pushed him to write even the most obscure bureaucratic memo with a refinement and dedication unheard of in the genre. In one of his most celebrated essays, *Defensa de la carta misiva y de la correspondencia epistolar* (A defense of the letter and letter writing) (1947), he put forward the idea that a letter is always a document of intimacy, always searching for a reader—"su encanto específico y su razón de lectura" (its specific charm and the reason for reading it).[7] Public knowledge and the distribution of private letters is essential in exploring the work of a writer with such diverse activities; in letter writing, voice and inscription become very comparable, and complete a dialectical relationship between two forces: presence and absence. Pedro Salinas became a master of this operation of enhancing absence through presence on the printed page, relating lived life and a written one. Writing letters became for him a way of establishing this continuity. On one occasion, in 1931, reporting to Jorge Guillén about a lecture tour he had done in Europe, he said, "Esto ya no era viaje, era vida con fondo de viaje" (This was not a trip, but life lived as a trip).[8] Perhaps unintentionally, he was

6. Claudio Guillén, "Pedro Salinas, múltiple," in *De leyendas y lecciones: Siglos XIX, XX y XXI* (Barcelona: Editorial Crítica, 2007), 105–43.

7. Pedro Salinas, "El Defensor: Ensayos," in *Ensayos Completos: Obras Completas II*, ed. Enric Bou and Andrés Soria Olmedo (Madrid: Cátedra, 2007), 887.

8. Salinas, *Epistolario Completo*, 264.

anticipating his future life in exile, and the importance that letter writing would have as a survival tool, as life insurance, or as a return ticket to some enchanted islands within the realm of literature.

Salinas's contribution to literary criticism may be read under the light and principles of the New Criticism, with emphasis on the text itself, not its paraphrase into critical jargons. His idea of literature is somewhat atemporal, always searching for eternal values, the essence of human beings. When speculating about his activity as a professor or literary critic, Salinas would stress the fact that he always wanted to explain "great works" as examples of eternal human values that still reflect present day situations and tribulations. He did not perceive old texts as some sort of arcane papyrus that critics and scholars should ornament with sophisticated and intricate footnotes (in a Nabokovian *Pale Fire* way), but rather as a *live* text. Thus younger generations of readers could remain sensitive to old texts as "live" or "living" words. He hoped that readers could remain attracted to writing from all eras, visualizing in them aesthetic, historic, moral, and philological issues related to their own lives. On many occasions, Salinas scorned his colleagues who refused to betray their true love for literature, and who chose to hide behind obscure data and elucidations. He would defend the pedagogical method of establishing a dialogue with the text and making it understandable for his students. This attitude of pointed transparency can also be seen in his approach to creative writing: Salinas wanted his own writings to be readily understood, and strived to create a mirror effect in the reader's mind through personal situations and feelings. At the same time, the poet was consciously fostering an ambiguity (and confusion) between life and literature. We can detect a Salinian concept, "phases of reality," that he learned from classical Spanish literature and incorporated into his own writing, especially in certain poems (particularly those from *My Voice Because of You*), in the plays, and in the short stories.

Pedro Salinas thrived on observation and curiosity, and was always amazed at the wonders of the world he was living in. Ahead of his time while in Spain, he explored new ways of writing, new venues of literature. He was as much a critical observer of Madrid's literary milieu as an explorer of Europe and a "rediscoverer" of the Americas, where he found both happiness and refuge in difficult times. Salinas's writings reflect the wonder and fear of a man trapped between two worlds, two cultures, two languages, and two time periods. The preoccupations crystallized in his theater and prose, his poems and letters, capture the contradictory and complex hardships and demands of an uprooted generation of writers. He reacted fiercely against what he deemed the insane. He feared the A-Bomb and its implications for military and other dangerous and

[203]

oppressive applications. As a newcomer to a new world, the one being created at the onset of the Cold War, he denounced, from a humanistic old-world perspective, the shortcomings, defects, and contradictions of contemporary civilization. And still, while alert to the dehumanizing aspects of this new era he so well chronicled, the poet's voice would never cease to marvel at his new constellations of stars.

Enric Bou
Providence, Rhode Island

SELECTED BIBLIOGRAPHY

POETRY BY PEDRO SALINAS

Amor en vilo. Madrid: Ediciones La Tentativa Poética, 1933.

Antología de la poesía de Pedro Salinas: La sonrisa amaorosa. Edición de Luis Izquierdo. Barcelona: Ediciones Juan Grainca, 1985.

Antología poética. Selección y nota preliminar de Julio Cortázar. Madrid: Alianza Editorial, 1974. Reprint 2003.

Aventura poética: Antología. Edición de David L. Stixrude. Madrid: Cátedra, 1980.

Confianza: Poemas inéditos (1942–1944). Prólogo de Jorge Guillén. Edición preparada y corregida por Jorge Guillén y Juan Marichal. Madrid: Aguilar, 1955.

El contemplado: Tema con variaciones. Mexico: Stylo, 1949.

El contemplado: *Todo más claro y otros poemas.* Introducción y notas de Francisco Javier Díez de Revenga. Madrid: Castalia, 1996. Reprint, Edición de Montserrat Escartín Gual. Madrid: Visor Libros, 2004. Reprint, San Juan, PR: Ediciones Callejón, 2004.

Fábula y signo. Madrid: El Plutarco, 1931.

Largo lamento. Edición de Montserrat Escartín Gual. Barcelona: Crítica, 2005.

La voz a ti debida, poema. Madrid: Los Cuatro Vientos, Signo, 1933. Reprint, Buenos Aires: Editorial Losada,1954. Reprint, Buenos Aires: Editorial Losada, 1967.

La voz a ti debida, Razón de amor, Largo lamento. Edición de Montserrat Escartín Gual. Madrid: Cátedra, 1995. Reprint 2003.

La voz a ti debida y Razón de amor. Introducción y notas de Joaquín González Muela. Madrid: Editorial Castalia, 1969.

Pedro Salinas para niños. Edición de Solita Salinas. Madrid: Ediciones de la Torre, 1992.

Poemas escogidos. Edición de Jorge Guillén. Madrid: Aguilar, 1955.

Poesías completas (4 tomos editados). Edición de Solita Salinas. Madrid: Alianza, 1989–90.

Poesías completas. Preparada y revisada por Juan Marichal. Madrid: Aguilar, 1961.

Poesías completas. Prólogo de Jorge Guillén. Edición preparada por Soledad Salinas de Marichal. Barcelona: Barral Editores, 1975. Reprint, Barcelona: Seix-Barral, 1981. Reprint, Barcelona: Editorial Lumen, 2000.

Presagios. Madrid: Biblioteca de Índice, 1923.

Razon de amor. Madrid: Ediciones Cruz y Raya, 1936. Reprint, Buenos Aires: Editorial Losada,1952.

Seguro azar. Madrid: Revista de Occidente, 1929.

Todo más claro y otros poemas. Buenos Aires: Losada, 1950.

THEATER BY PEDRO SALINAS

Judit y el tirano: Comedia en tres actos. Madrid: Teatro Español, 1992.

La fuente del Arcángel. La bella durmiente. El director Caín o una gloria científica. Edición de Gregorio Torres Nebrera. Col. Bitácora, n. 66, 1979.

Teatro completo. Prólogo de Juan Marichal. Madrid: Aguilar, 1957. Reprint, edición de Pilar Moraleda. Sevilla: Alfar. Col. Universidad, 1979.

Teatro: La cabeza de Medusa. La estratoesfera. La isla del tesoro. Tres piezas dramáticas en un acto. Madrid, Insula, 1952.

NARRATIVE BY PEDRO SALINAS

El desnudo impeccable y otras narracions. Mexico: Tezontle, 1951.

La bomba increíble: Fabulación. Buenos Aires: Sudamericana, 1950. Reprint, Madrid: Aguilar, 1959. Reprint, prólogo de Andrés Soria Olmedo. Madrid: Viamonte, 1997.

Narrativa completa. Edición de Solita Salinas. Barcelona: Barral, 1976.

Prelude to Pleasure: A Bilingual Edition of Víspera del gozo. Translated by Noël Valis. Lewisburg: Bucknell University Press; London: Associated University Presses, 1993.

Víspera del gozo. Madrid: Revista de Occidente, 1926. Reprint, Madrid: Alianza Editorial, 1974.

LETTERS BY PEDRO SALINAS

Cartas a Katherine Whitmore, 1932–1947. Edición y prólogo de Enric Bou. Barcelona: Tusquets Editores, 2002.

Cartas de amor a Margarita, 1912–1915. Edición de Solita Salinas. Madrid: Alianza.

Cartas de viaje: 1912–1951. Edición, prólogo y notas de Enric Bou. Valencia : Pre-textos, 1996.

Correspondencia con Guillén, 1923–1951. Edición de Andrés Soria Olmedo. Barcelona: Tusquets, 1992.

CRITICISM BY PEDRO SALINAS

El defensor. Madrid: Alianza,1967. Reprint 1954.

El romancismo y el siglo XX. Paris: Librairie des éditions espagnoles,1955.

Ensayos de literatura hispánica: Del «Cantar de Mio Cid» a García Lorca. Edición y prólogo de Juan Marichal. Madrid: Aguilar, 1967.

Jorge Manrique: Tradición y originalidad. Barcelona: Ediciones Península, 2003.

La gran Cabeza de Turco o la minoría literaria. Mexico, 1946.

La poesía de Rubén Darío: Ensayo sobre el tema y los temas del poeta. Barcelona: Ediciones Península, 2005.

La realidad y el poeta. Versión castellana y edición a cargo de Soledad Salinas de Marichal. Barcelona: Ariel, 1976.

La responsabilidad del escritor. Barcelona: Seix Barral, 1964.

Literatura española siglo XX. Madrid: Alianza Editorial, 2000.

Reality and the Poet in Spanish Poetry. Baltimore: Johns Hopkins Press, 1966.

Significación del Esperpento o Valle Inclán, Hijo Predilecto [Prodigo] del 98. México, 1947.

EDITIONS BY PEDRO SALINAS OF OTHER AUTHORS

Luis, de Granada (1504–1588). Maravilla del mundo. Selección y prólogo de Pedro Salinas. México: Editorial Séneca, 1940.

Meléndez Valdés, Juan (1754–1817). Poesías: Edición, prólogo y notas de Pedro Salinas. Madrid: Espasa-Calpe, 1955.

Poema de mío Cid: Puesto en romance vulgar y lenguaje moderno por Pedro Salinas. Madrid: Revista de Occidente, 1926.

Poetas del 27: Antología comentada. Introducción, Víctor García de la Concha. Madrid: Editorial Espasa Calpe, 1998.

San Juan de la Cruz (Saint John of the Cross): Poesías completas. Edición, prólogo y notas de Pedro Salinas. Santiago de Chile: Cruz del Sur, 1947.

TRANSLATIONS OF THE POETRY

Certain Chance: Poems. Versions and introduction by David Lee Garrison, prologue by Pedro Salinas, reminiscence by Willis Barnstone, art by David Leach. Lewisburg: Bucknell University Press; London: Associated University Presses, 2000.

The Lost Angel and Other Poems. Translated by Eleanor Turnbull. Baltimore: The Johns Hopkins Press, 1938.

My Voice Because of You [La voz a ti debida]. Translation and introduction by Willis Barnstone. Preface by Jorge Guillén. Albany: State University of New York Press, 1976.

Sea of San Juan: A Contemplation. Translated by Eleanor Turnbull. Boston: Humphries, 1950.

To Live in Pronouns: Selected Love Poems. Translated by Edith Helman and Norma Farber. New York: Norton, 1974.

Truth of Two, and Other Poems. Translated by Eleanor Turnbull. Baltimore: The Johns Hopkins Press, 1940

STUDIES

Allen, Rupert C. *Symbolic Experience: A Study of Poems by Pedro Salinas*. Tuscaloosa: University of Alabama Press, 1982.

Barnstone, Willis. "Telephone Meditations in *My Voice Because of You*," in *The Poetics of Ecstasy: Varieties of Ekstasis from Sappho to Borges*. New York: Holmes and Meir, 1983.

Barrera López, José María. *El azar impecable: Vida y obra de Pedro Salinas*. Sevilla: Alcalá de Guadaira; Sevilla: Editorial Guadalmena, 1993.

Berbenni, Gino. *La poesia di Pedro Salinas*. Padova: Rebellato, 1967.

Cirre, José Francisco. *El mundo lírico de Pedro Salinas*. Granada: Editorial Don Quijote, 1982.

Costa Viva, Olga. *Pedro Salinas frente a la realidad*. Madrid: Alfaguara, 1969.

Crispin, John. *Pedro Salinas*. New York: Twayne Publishers, 1974.

Darmangeat, Pierre. *Pedro Salinas et La voz a ti debida*. Paris: Éditions espagnoles, 1955.

Dehennin, Else. *Passion d'absolu et tension expressive dans l'oeuvre de Pedro Salinas*. Ghent: Romanica Gandensia, 1957.

Feal Deibe, Carlos. *La poesía de Pedro Salinas*. Madrid: Editorial Gredos, 1965.

———. *Poesía y narrativa de Pedro Salinas*. Madrid: Gredos, 2000.

Hartfield-Méndez, Vialla. *Woman and the Infinite: Epiphanic Moments in Pedro Salinas's Art*. Lewisburg: Bucknell University Press; London: Associated University Presses; Cranbury, NJ: Associated University Presses, 1996.

Nebrera, Gregorio Torres. *Teatro: Estudio, notas y comentarios de text*. Madrid: Narcea, D.L., 1979.

Newman, Jean Cross. *Pedro Salinas y su circunstancia: Biografía*. Prólogo de Jorge Guillén. Traducción de Rosa Cifuentes. Madrid: Páginas de Espuma, 2004.

Orringer, Stephanie L. *Pedro Salinas' Theater of Self-Authentication*. New York: P. Lang, 1995.

Palley, Julian. *La luz no usada: La poesía de Pedro Salinas*. México: Ediciones de Andrea, 1966.

Ramírez de Arellano, Diana. *Caminos de la creación poética en Pedro Salinas*. Madrid: Romo Arregui, 1956.

Spitzer, Leo, and Angel del Rio. *Vida y obra*, por Ángel del Río; *El conceptismo interior de Pedro Salinas*, por Leo Spitzer. New York: Hispanic Institute in the United States, 1942.

Vila Selma, José. *Pedro Salinas*. Madrid: Epesa, 1972.

Zubizarreta, Alma de. *Pedro Salinas: El diálogo creador*. Prólogo de Jorge Guillén. Madrid: Editorial Gredos, 1969.

INDEX OF FIRST LINES